The Key Vocabulary Routine

Second Edition

Joan Sedita

Keys to Literacy®

319 Newburyport Tpke, Suite 205
Rowley, MA 01969
978-948-8511 www.keystoliteracy.com

Edited by Meg Crossan, Sue Nichols, Kathe Simons
Cover design and text layout: Peggy MacNeil

ISBN 0-9786106-1-X

Printed in the United States of America

Published and Distributed by

Keys to Literacy®

319 Newburyport Tpke, Suite 205
Rowley, MA 01969
978-948-8511 www.keystoliteracy.com

Big Words for Little People
Today I fee Silly Jaime Lee Curtis

Weighted Word Book

Max's Words

Dedication

To Rosalie, my mother, who gave me my first words.

Acknowledgements

The Key Vocabulary Routine is the result of many years of work with students and teachers around vocabulary instruction. I would like to thank all of the teachers who have participated in my professional development sessions and provided feedback about the content in *The Key Vocabulary Routine*.

I am grateful to all of my colleagues who have supported my efforts to identify vocabulary instruction that works and to develop this routine for teachers. Specifically I would like to thank Becky DeSmith and Shauna Cotte at Keys to Literacy for piloting *The Key Vocabulary Routine* – their contributions were essential to the content of the book and training model. I am very grateful to Sue Nichols who helped edit and shepherd this book from draft to publication. Thanks also to Alex Coakley and Peggy MacNeil for their work on book layout and printing and to my colleagues who reviewed the first draft. I would especially like to thank my partner at Keys to Literacy and longtime friend, Brad Neuenhaus, for encouraging me to develop *The Key Vocabulary Routine* and write this book and for helping me build Keys to Literacy. Finally, I would like to thank my husband, Joe DelGuidice, for always supporting my work but reminding me to also smell the roses.

Bringing Words To Life

Robust Vocabulary

TABLE OF CONTENTS

PART II: The Five Steps in The Key Vocabulary Routine

Step 1: Preview for Difficult Vocabulary

Step 2: Use Activities to Connect Vocabulary

Step 3: Select Specific Words to Teach In-Depth

Step 4: Identify Opportunities to Teach Word Learning Strategies

Step 5: Promote Word Consciousness

Introduction

The Key Vocabulary Routine integrates research-based activities into content classroom instruction. By previewing words before students read, selecting key words to teach in-depth, using activities that help students connect words, and teaching use of context and word analysis to determine the meaning of unknown words, teachers help students acquire new words and build their vocabularies.

The information in this book is organized into two parts:

- **Part I: Overview of Comprehension and Vocabulary Instruction**
  - **Chapter 1** explains *The Key Vocabulary Routine* and the advantage of having a routine that is consistent as students move from grade to grade and class to class. This chapter also summarizes how students learn words using the routine and basic teaching principles such as explicit instruction, gradual release of responsibility, scaffolding, spiraling back, and differentiated instruction.

  - **Chapter 2** identifies vocabulary as one of five components of reading, reviews the connection between vocabulary knowledge and comprehension, and summarizes how students build their vocabularies over time. This chapter also reviews the research on effective practices for teaching vocabulary.

- **Part II: The Five Steps in The Key Vocabulary Routine**

  - **Step 1:** Preview for difficult vocabulary

  - **Step 2:** Use activities to connect vocabulary to background knowledge and related words

  - **Step 3:** Select specific words to teach in-depth

  - **Step 4:** Identify opportunities to teach word learning strategies

  - **Step 5:** Promote word consciousness

A section at the end of the book includes reproducible templates that can be copied and used in the classroom with students.

Part 1

Overview of Comprehension and Vocabulary Instruction

What is The Key Vocabulary Routine?

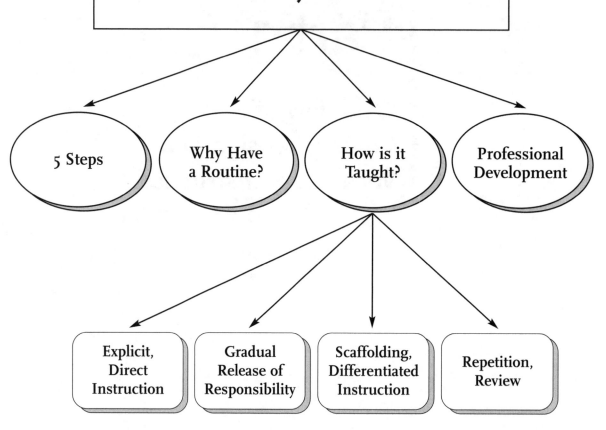

- 5 Steps
- Why Have a Routine?
- How is it Taught?
- Professional Development

How is it Taught?
- Explicit, Direct Instruction
- Gradual Release of Responsibility
- Scaffolding, Differentiated Instruction
- Repetition, Review

Chapter 1

What is The Key Vocabulary Routine?

The Key Vocabulary Routine is a program for teaching content vocabulary in grades three through twelve that can be used in all classrooms and subject areas. The program emphasizes the integration of vocabulary instruction using existing content teaching materials (i.e., textbooks and other reading material) taught by teachers in all subject areas (e.g., science, social studies, English Language Arts, math).

Consistent with the research findings that there is no single best way to teach vocabulary, *The Key Vocabulary Routine* emphasizes both direct and indirect methods for building students' vocabulary. Also consistent with the research findings that there is no single best time to teach vocabulary, *The Key Vocabulary Routine* is intended to be used in content classrooms throughout the day. In fact, content teachers are often in the best position to determine which content-specific words are most worth teaching in their subject area.

Vocabulary instruction experts recommend a multi-component approach to teach vocabulary. *The Key Vocabulary Routine* uses a set of foundational steps to create a routine that teachers can use on a consistent basis. When *The Key Vocabulary Routine* is used by a team of teachers who work with the same students, across a grade level or on a school-wide basis, students are exposed to vocabulary instruction that is consistent and persistent from grade to grade and class to class. It is a systematic program that connects what we know from the research about best practices to daily, classroom instruction.

There are five steps in *The Key Vocabulary Routine* (see Figure B). Part II of this book is organized around these five steps.

Breadth and Depth of Word Knowledge

In order to sufficiently grow student vocabulary knowledge, vocabulary instruction must focus on both **breadth** and **depth**. The goal of broad instruction is exposure to many words, and the goal of deep instruction is in-depth teaching of a smaller set of words. Figure A illustrates the combination of these goals. The steps in *The Key Vocabulary Routine* address both breadth and depth. Step 1 (Preview) and Step 5 (Word Consciousness) provide broad knowledge of many words; Step 2 (Word Connections), Step 3 (Select Words to Teach In-Depth), and Step 4 (Word Learning Strategies) provide deep knowledge of specific words.

Figure A

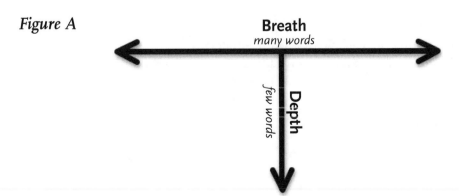

Why Do Content Classroom Teachers Need a Routine?

A significant body of research exists identifying the most effective practices for teaching vocabulary and helping students grow their vocabularies. However, much of this research has not found its way into content classrooms. There is still too much reliance on traditional instructional approaches that are not very effective, such as having students look up, copy, and memorize definitions, and non-cognitive activities such as matching definitions or fill-in-the-blank. Teachers also rely too much on textbook publishers to identify key vocabulary for direct teaching. The first reason to use a routine such as *The Key Vocabulary Routine* is to ensure that teachers base their vocabulary instruction on best practice.

A second reason is to provide a basic set of foundational activities that, through repetition and consistent use by all teachers, students can learn easily and use independently. There are numerous books for teachers about how to teach vocabulary, and a quick search of the internet yields hundreds of vocabulary templates, graphic

Figure B

The Key Vocabulary Routine

1. Preview for difficult vocabulary
   - Identify problematic words, phrases, figurative language
   - Generate a previewing list
   - Provide background knowledge about the words to aid in comprehension while reading

2. Use activities that connect vocabulary to background knowledge and related words
   - Categorizing
   - Semantic Mapping
   - Semantic Feature Analysis
   - Scaling

3. Select specific words to teach in-depth
   - Identify a small set of key content words
   - Teach all aspects of the words
   - Develop user-friendly definitions

4. Identify opportunities to teach word learning strategies
   - Use of context to determine word meaning
   - Use of word parts to determine word meaning

5. Promote word consciousness

organizers, and teaching tips. With so many options, teachers can feel overwhelmed by the choices, and students become confused when they must learn how to use different formats, strategies, and activities for multiple teachers. *The Key Vocabulary Routine* provides a standard routine so students can focus on learning new vocabulary rather than new activities.

Students have many, many words to learn across the curriculum; a vocabulary routine must happen during every content class, not just in the English Language Arts class. Also, content area vocabulary is often different and unique from vocabulary that students encounter in literature. There are three ways that content area vocabulary may be different from vocabulary in literature (Armbruster & Nagy, 1992; Billmeyer & Barton, 1998):

1. Content vocabulary consists of major concept words that are essential to understanding the information associated with specific subjects.

2. Content vocabulary is often not associated with words that students already know from everyday conversation. There is no prior knowledge or even synonyms for many content specific words. On the other hand, words encountered in literature may already be familiar to students.

3. Content area vocabulary words are often related in meaning, affording opportunities to learn new words in connection with other words. With literature, it is often harder to make connections between unfamiliar words.

Many content-area textbooks include specialized vocabulary and discipline-related concepts that students may not encounter elsewhere. Explicit instruction in specialized, content vocabulary such as in science or social studies has been identified as an important way to contribute to successful reading comprehension among adolescent students, and it enhances their ability to acquire textbook vocabulary (Kamil et al., 2008).

Another reason to use *The Key Vocabulary Routine* is that the content teacher, rather than a textbook publisher, decides which words to teach based on the needs of the students and the content. While it may be helpful when textbooks highlight specific words, teachers should not solely rely on the text to identify words to teach. Step 3 in *The Key Vocabulary Routine* addresses how teachers can identify the content words to provide direct instruction based on the particular background knowledge of their students, the various reading material that will be used, and the emphasis on certain content topics that will be covered in class.

A final reason to use *The Key Vocabulary Routine* is that it emphasizes daily, integrated vocabulary instruction. A number of schools continue to purchase vocabulary programs that consist of pre-determined weekly lists of words that students are expected to learn. Typically these programs include workbooks with activities that are designed to help students memorize definitions for the word list (i.e., flash cards, matching, fill-in-the-blank). Often these vocabulary programs are used only in the English Language Arts class during a specific time designated for vocabulary instruction. Unfortunately, this approach runs counter to the research on effective vocabulary instruction. Instead, vocabulary instruction should be tied to and woven into content instruction throughout the school day. Because *The Key Vocabulary Routine* is used in the content classroom, all teachers can take advantage of opportunities that arise to incorporate effective vocabulary instruction.

How is *The Key Vocabulary Routine* Taught?

There are several instructional practices, or teaching principles, that enable teachers to meet a wide variety of learning styles and needs when they are teaching vocabulary. Collectively, these principles are the hallmark of differentiated instruction. Teachers should provide explicit and direct instruction in why, how, and when to apply vocabulary strategies. Significant modeling, guided practice, and opportunities to practice application of vocabulary strategies are critical. Each of these principles is described in detail below.

Explicit and Direct Instruction

To become good readers, most students need explicit, direct instruction (National Reading Panel, 2000). Research indicates that direct teaching of specific words and word-learning strategies can both add words to students' vocabularies and improve reading comprehension of texts containing those words (Lehr et al., 2004). Explicit reading strategy instruction includes explaining what a given strategy is, why it is important, and when to use the strategy. Using a classroom text, the teacher models the strategy, helps students learn how to apply it, and guides students as they try the strategy on their own (Texas Reading Initiative, 2000).

Direct instruction as it relates to vocabulary includes teaching both specific words and word learning strategies, such as using the context and knowledge of word parts to help determine the meaning of a new word. It also includes direct instruction in how to use a dictionary.

Gradual Release of Responsibility

The Gradual Release of Responsibility Model (Pearson & Gallagher, 1983) is an effective approach for teaching vocabulary words and strategies. This can be described as an *I do it, we do it, you do it* model of instruction (see Figure C). Using this model, the teacher presents a strategy to the class and shows how the strategy is used, including "thinking aloud" *(I do it)*. For example, when teaching word parts, the teacher might point out how the root of several related words is the same (e.g., *phon* means sound as in *telephone, symphony,* and *phonograph*).

The teacher then has the students practice applying the strategy as a group (*we do it*). Continuing with the example above, the teacher might provide a list of common roots and ask students as a whole or in small collaborative groups to generate examples of related words that have the same root. Finally, students independently try applying their knowledge of roots and prefixes/suffixes to determine the meaning of unfamiliar words (*you do it*).

Figure C

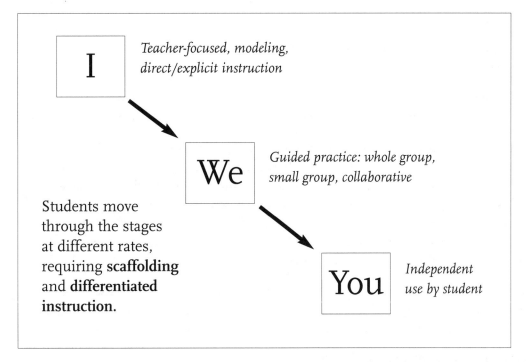

Many students need significant guided practice at the *we do it* stage in order to move on to independent use of a strategy (*you do it*). The National Reading Panel (2000) found that when peers instruct or interact over the use of reading comprehension strategies, it increases the use of these strategies and improves reading comprehension. *The Key Vocabulary Routine* incorporates the use of whole- and small-group collaboration activities to help students learn strategies such as: connecting new words to related words through categorizing, semantic mapping, semantic feature analysis, and scaling activities; using the context to determine word meaning; and using knowledge of word parts.

Scaffolding and Differentiated Instruction

The term scaffold is used to describe "teacher support of a learner through dialogue, questioning, conversation, and non-verbal modeling, in which the learner attempts literacy tasks that could not be done without assistance" (Peterson et al., 2000, pp. 17-18). Scaffolding centers on the notion of providing struggling readers with support as they learn to read. Research indicates that scaffolding must take place across the curriculum, and that reading strategies that are not supported by content teachers have little chance of being transferred by struggling secondary readers (Gaskins, 1998).

Dickson, Simmons, and Kame'enui (1995) suggest four types of scaffolding:

> **Teacher/peer scaffolding.** Occurs across the continuum, with more support occurring when new concepts, tasks, or strategies are introduced. Support is gradually decreased as students gain proficiency and assume more responsibility.

Content scaffolding. Occurs as the teacher first introduces simpler concepts and skills and then slowly guides students through more challenging concepts and skills.

Task scaffolding. Occurs as the student proceeds from easier to more difficult tasks and activities.

Material scaffolding. Occurs when a variety of materials are used to guide student thinking, including partially completed graphic organizers or templates.

Differentiated instruction is supported when a teacher proactively plans varied approaches to what students need to learn, how they will learn it, and how they can express what they have learned so they can learn as much as efficiently as possible (Tomlinson, 2003). It means designing instruction based on individual student needs rather than on a standardized approach to instruction that assumes all students learn the same way. The use of scaffolding while teaching vocabulary, therefore, requires the teacher to apply a differentiated approach to instruction.

Because some students have more advanced vocabularies than others and some may become proficient at applying vocabulary strategies sooner than others, scaffolding and differentiated instruction are essential for every step in *The Key Vocabulary Routine*.

Mastery Through Repetition and Review

When students learn information or a word at an *automatic* level, it means they have learned it so thoroughly that they can use it with little or no conscious attention (Sedita, 1989). Information must be at an automatic level, or mastery level, for it to be used as a foundation to learn something new. Practice is the key to becoming automatic, and the more new and novel the information, the more repeated exposure and practice it takes to become automatic.

The brain is constantly changing and does not hold on to new information if it is not related to something to which the brain has already connected. The brain needs frequent exposure to information or a word to build lasting memory (Jensen, 2005). Repeated exposure is more likely if teachers make conscious decisions to spiral back over previously learned information and words. Showing the connection between current material and material learned last week or last month will help ensure automaticity and long-term memory.

The Key Vocabulary Routine for Primary Grades

The Key Vocabulary Routine was designed for use with students in grades 3-12. However, many of the instructional practices from the routine can also be used to grow the vocabulary of students in kindergarten through second grade. Several classroom examples from these primary grades are provided at the end of the book. We suggest the following instructional modification for use of the routine with younger students:

- Provide significantly more opportunities for students to listen to rich language through read aloud and modeling by the teacher.

- Provide opportunities for students to talk among themselves to practice using the new words they are learning.

- Complete the activities used in Step 2 of the routine through discussion rather than reading and writing the words (i.e., semantic feature analysis, semantic mapping, categorizing, scaling).

- In Step 3 of the routine, focus more on Tier 2 words (in Beck and McKeown's Three Tier Model) to teach in-depth.

- In Step 4 of the routine, introduce use of context during read alouds. Develop morphological awareness by teaching students how to create compound words and add simple prefixes and suffixes to short Anglo-Saxon words (rather than Greek and Latin roots).

Professional Development For The Key Vocabulary Routine

The National Reading Panel (2000) found that professional development is essential for teachers to develop knowledge of reading comprehension strategies. The RAND Reading Study Group (Snow, 2002) further noted that recent studies have underscored the importance of teacher preparation as a way to deliver effective instruction in reading comprehension strategies, especially when the students are low performing.

Professional development must be efficient and relate directly to what teachers are doing in their classrooms. Teachers need a basic routine that can be applied easily to any reading and content material. In addition, given the limited budgets facing most schools today, it is essential that vocabulary instruction be integrated using existing classroom reading material.

The Key Vocabulary Routine is flexible, can be used in all content classrooms, and does not require the purchase of additional instructional materials. Teachers use their knowledge of research-based best practices to teach vocabulary using their own classroom materials.

Research also indicates that in order for teachers to use strategies effectively, extensive follow up professional development is necessary (National Reading Panel, 2000; Snow, 2002). In order to be successful and long lasting, initial training must be followed by sustained opportunities to practice the application of the training with the support of a professional trainer, a building based coach, and peer support. The goal should be to gradually eliminate the need for a professional trainer as soon as possible.

Professional development for *The Key Vocabulary Routine* is provided by Keys to Literacy. It includes initial training, the training of building-based coaches, and on-site follow-up with small groups of teachers when a Keys to Literacy trainer facilitates peer interaction and implementation of the program. The recommended professional development model for implementing *The Key Vocabulary Routine* includes the following:

- **A two-day initial training:** Using this book, initial training reviews the research on effective vocabulary instruction and introduces each of the steps in the Routine. Teachers bring classroom reading material to the training so they can practice generating vocabulary activities using their own instructional material. At the end of the training, teachers are given implementation portfolios to use for keeping a log of activity use. They save examples of classroom vocabulary lessons and student work samples in the portfolios to share later at follow-up meetings.

- **Training of building-based Key Vocabulary coaches:** One or more individuals from a school become peer coaches for *The Key Vocabulary Routine*. They attend a Keys to Literacy sponsored two-day coach training where they learn how to support the implementation of *The Key Vocabulary Routine* and offer help to their peers.

- **Follow-up support for teachers:** A Keys to Literacy trainer conducts small-group meetings on-site at schools. Teachers bring their implementation portfolios and share with their peers the activities and student work from their classrooms. The trainer provides feedback and facilitates the sharing of ideas. If necessary, the trainer reviews the steps, methods, and components of vocabulary instruction and offers guided practice. The building coaches attend these meetings so they can learn how to facilitate peer meetings. At least three follow-up meetings are recommended, scheduled approximately every four to six weeks after initial training.

- **Guided practice sessions:** Guided practice sessions conducted by a Keys to Literacy trainer are also available on-site at schools. During these sessions, teachers have an opportunity to practice generating vocabulary lessons and activities with support from the trainer.

For further details about professional development for *The Key Vocabulary Routine*, contact Keys to Literacy on-line at www.keystoliteracy.com, by phone (978-948-8511) or by email (info@keystoliteracy.com)

NOTES:

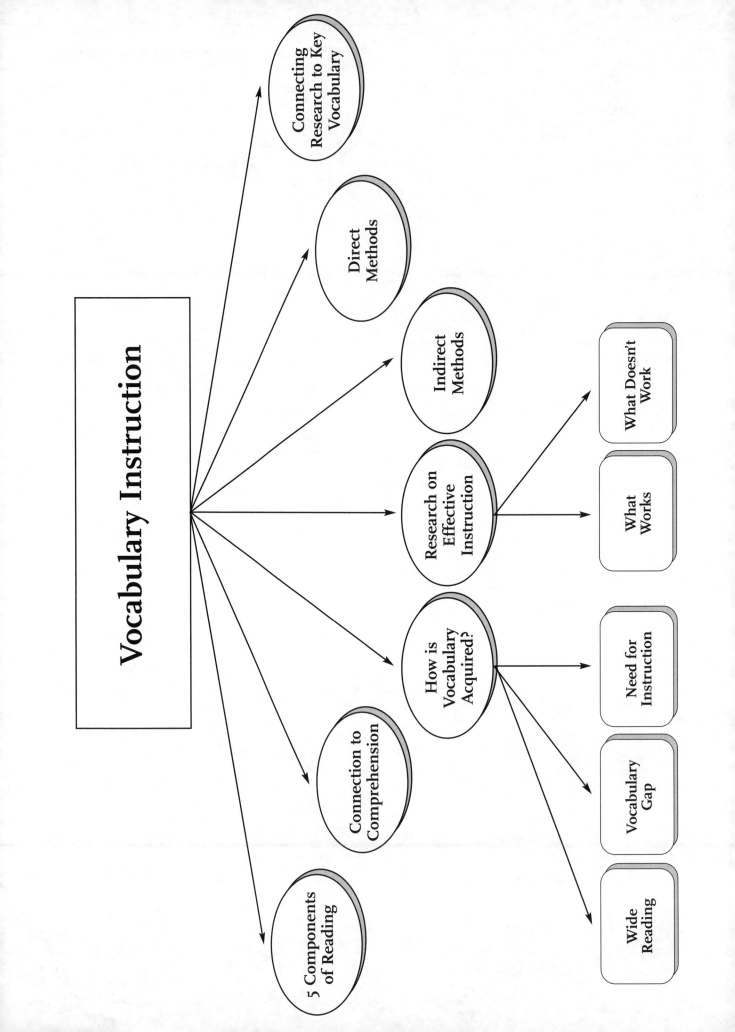

Chapter 2

Vocabulary Instruction

Why is vocabulary instruction important? Vocabulary knowledge encompasses all the words we must know to access our background knowledge, express our ideas and communicate them to others, and learn new concepts. Students' word knowledge is linked strongly to general academic success because students who have large vocabularies can understand new concepts more quickly than students with limited vocabularies.

Vocabulary instruction is necessary because of the vast number of words students must acquire each year in order to read and understand grade-level text. If students do not adequately and steadily build their vocabulary knowledge, reading comprehension will be affected (Chall & Jacobs, 2003). Estimates vary of how many words students must learn every year, ranging from 2,000 – 3,500 words per year after grade three (Anderson & Nagy, 1992; Beck & McKeown, 1991). The number of words high school graduates need to know is estimated to be between 60,000 to 100,000 (Hirsch, 2006).

However, there are huge discrepancies in the number of words that students may know. Beck, McKeown, and Kucan note the following in their book *Bringing Words to Life: Robust Vocabulary Instruction* (2002):

- First grade children from higher socioeconomic groups know about twice as many words as children from lower socioeconomic groups.

- High school seniors near the top of their class know about four times as many words as their lower-performing classmates.

- High-knowledge third graders have vocabularies about equal to the lowest-performing 12th graders.

For students who are English language learners (ELL), vocabulary instruction is essential. Because these students acquire English vocabulary later, they often enter school with fewer words than their English-speaking peers. Research has found that ELL students are capable of eventually matching or even transcending native speaker levels of vocabulary knowledge, especially if they are exposed to vocabulary through a great deal of reading. There is also evidence that the same instructional practices that promote vocabulary learning in students with English as their primary language also promote vocabulary for ELL students (Snow & Kim, 2007).

Activity 1: Current Vocabulary Instruction Practices
Directions: Use the questions below for a small-group discussion about current practices in your school.

How do you teach vocabulary?

_____

_____

_____

_____

_____

_____

Does your school use a formal vocabulary program or a consistent approach for teaching vocabulary?

_____

_____

_____

_____

_____

_____

Make a list of activities you use that seem to improve your students' vocabulary.

_____

_____

_____

_____

_____

_____

Vocabulary: One of Five Components of Reading

There are five components of instruction that must be addressed to successfully teach students to read and comprehend (National Reading Panel, 2000):

Phonemic Awareness: The ability to notice, think about, and work with the individual sounds in spoken words. Before students learn to read, they must understand how the sounds in words work.

Phonics: The ability to understand the relationship between the letters of written language and the individual sounds of spoken language. Also, the use of letter combinations and patterns, syllable types, and word attack skills to read and spell words.

Fluency: The ability to read text quickly, accurately, and automatically, with proper expression and understanding.

Vocabulary: The ability to understand the meaning of words. Vocabulary is a crucial component for reading comprehension.

Comprehension: To derive meaning from the text based on the information in the text in combination with the reader's own knowledge. Comprehension can be improved by teaching students to use specific reading strategies. These include pre-reading skills, note taking, generating and answering questions, developing graphic organizers and story maps, and summarizing.

The first three components (Phonemic Awareness, Phonics, and Fluency) constitute basic decoding and encoding skills. Combined, they produce readers who can identify and spell words accurately and fluently. The ultimate goal of reading, however, is to understand what is read. The last two components (Vocabulary and Comprehension) enable readers to construct meaning once words are identified. See Figure A.

Figure A

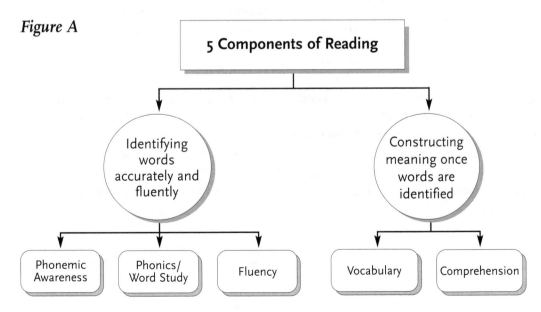

The Connection between Vocabulary Knowledge and Comprehension

One of the oldest findings in educational research is the strong relationship between vocabulary knowledge and reading comprehension. Word knowledge is crucial to determining how well students will be able to understand the texts they read. Comprehension is far more than recognizing words and remembering their meanings. However, if a student does not know the meanings of a sufficient proportion of the words in text, comprehension is impossible.

A complete plan for teaching comprehension should include instruction in four components: vocabulary, comprehension strategies, text structure, and background knowledge (see Figure B). *The Key Vocabulary Routine* primarily addresses vocabulary, but it also addresses to some degree background knowledge and comprehension strategies. *The Key Comprehension Routine* (Sedita, 2010) is a professional development program that addresses text structure and comprehension strategy instruction. The program combines three key skills (main idea, note taking, summarizing) into a set of basic strategy activities that can be used with any subject matter. Information about this program is available at Keys to Literacy (www.keystoliteracy.com). Together, *The Key Vocabulary Routine* and *The Key Comprehension Routine* provide a total program for improving students' reading comprehension.

Figure B

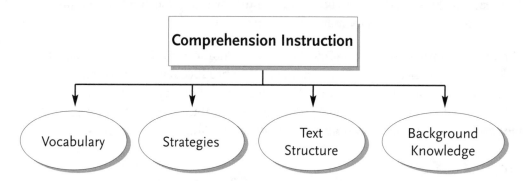

Vocabulary experts agree that students should know between 90 and 95 percent of the words in a text to fully understand what they are reading (Stahl, 1999; Samuels, 2002). Knowing at least 90 percent of the words enables readers to get the main idea and guess correctly what many unfamiliar words mean, which will help students learn new words. Readers who do not recognize at least 90 percent of the vocabulary will not only have difficulty comprehending the text, but they will also miss out on the opportunity to learn new words.

Activity 2: Simulation

Directions: Twenty percent of the vocabulary words have been omitted from this passage. Read the passage and answer the questions.

Just then the ___ line came ___ under his foot, where he had kept a ___ of the line, and he dropped his ___ and felt the ___ of the small ___ ___ pull as he held the line ___ and ___ to ___ it in.

The ___ ___ as he pulled in and he could see the blue back of the fish in the ___ and the ___ of his sides before he ___ him over the side and into the boat. He ___ in the ___ in the sun, ___ and bullet ___, his big, ___ eyes ___ as he thumped his life out against the ___ of the boat with the quick ___ ___ of his neat, fast-moving tail.

From: The Old Man And The Sea by Ernest Hemingway

Questions:

1. What do you think this passage is about?

_____

_____

_____

_____

2. What did it feel like to read this passage without knowing some of the vocabulary words?

_____

_____

_____

_____

3. Did you apply any strategies to help you make meaning from the passage?

_____

_____

_____

_____

(Note: The full passage may be found at the end of this chapter)

How Do Students Acquire New Vocabulary?

While there are a number of direct and indirect instructional practices that can be used in school to grow the vocabularies of students, the main way that all children, teenagers, and adults learn new words is through exposure to oral and written language.

Before entering school, word learning takes place through listening to those around us. The more exposure preschoolers have to rich oral language experiences, the greater their knowledge of vocabulary. Once in school, most of the words young children hear are words they already know. Beginning in grade three the source for learning new words shifts to written context through reading; many more new words are encountered through the written word versus the spoken word. However, because written text does not offer features of oral language such as intonation, body language, and shared physical surroundings, it is more difficult to learn new words from reading (Beck, et al., 2002). Figure C illustrates the significant difference in the amount of exposure to new words that are encountered in written language (i.e., various levels of text) and spoken language (i.e., television and adult speech).

Figure C

Selected Statistics for Major Sources of Spoken and Written Language (Sample Means)

	Rare Words Per 1,000
I. Printed texts	
Abstracts of scientific articles	128.0
Newspapers	68.3
Popular magazines	65.7
Adult books	52.7
Comic books	53.5
Children's books	30.9
Preschool books	16.3
II. Television texts	
Popular prime-time adult shows	22.7
Popular prime-time children's shows	20.2
Cartoon shows	30.8
Mr. Rogers and *Sesame Street*	2.0
III. Adult speech	
Expert witness testimony	28.4
College graduates to friends, spouses	17.3

Adapted from: Hayes, D.P., & Ahrens, M. (1988). Vocabulary simplification for children: A special case of "Motherese." *Journal of child language*, 15, 401.

The Need for Wide Reading

The amount students read is strongly related to their vocabulary knowledge (National Reading Panel, 2000). Students learn new words by encountering them in text, either by being read to or through their own reading. Increasing the opportunities to be exposed to new words improves students' vocabulary knowledge, which in turn improves their ability to read and understand more complex text. Providing opportunities for wide reading should be an essential part of a vocabulary curriculum.

Wide reading includes the number of words read and the amount of time spent reading. Wide reading also includes the exposure to a broad variety of genres in varied topics at different levels that will provide the kind of multiple exposures and background knowledge that are needed to effectively learn new words.

The following chart (Figure D) is based on data from Anderson & Nagy (1992). It shows the huge difference in exposure to words between those students who read a lot each day and those who do not.

Figure D

Minutes Per Day Spent Reading Outside of School	Words Read Per Year in Books
65.0	4,358,000
21.2	1,823,000
14.2	1,146,000
9.6	622,000
6.5	432,000
4.6	282,000
3.2	200,000
1.8	106,000
.7	21,000
.1	8,000

Adapted from: Anderson, R.C., & Nagy, W.E. (1992). "The vocabulary conundrum." *American Educator,* 16 (4); 14-18, 44-47.

Reading aloud can be a good way to expose students to written text to learn new vocabulary. Stahl, Richek, and Vandevier (1991) found that sixth-grade students learned word meanings from a read-aloud at the same rate that students typically learned words from written context. They suggest that listening to stories can be a rich source of word learning. Listening may substitute for some of the lack of reading by struggling readers and students with learning disabilities. However, listening to text read aloud cannot replace reading instruction.

The Gap in Vocabulary Knowledge Widens

Students vary in the word knowledge they bring to school. Their socioeconomic backgrounds and the language used in their homes and communities can influence opportunities to expand their vocabularies (Hart & Risley, 1995). Students who have more vocabulary knowledge in kindergarten become better readers than those who have limited vocabulary (National Institute for Literacy, 2001). These good readers tend to read more, which improves their reading skill and enables them to learn new words.

Students who have weak vocabularies have difficulty getting meaning from what they read. They find reading difficult and tedious, so they read less. As a result, they learn fewer words because they are not reading broadly enough to encounter and learn new words, and they fall behind compared to their peers. Unfortunately, the gap in vocabulary knowledge between good and poor readers tends to widen as they progress beyond third grade (Chall & Jacobs, 1983).

Why Vocabulary Instruction is Necessary in Addition to Wide Reading

Counting on wide reading to increase vocabulary knowledge is not enough to ensure good vocabulary growth in school. While incidental learning of new words through exposure to rich oral language and text is a major way for students to learn vocabulary, these incidental encounters cannot ensure that students will acquire in-depth meaning of specific words (Fukkink & de Glopper, 1998; Lehr et al., 2004).

All students, whether they have large or small vocabularies, benefit from vocabulary instruction (Beck et al., 1992). For some students, there are significant obstacles to developing sufficient vocabulary to be successful in school, and these students in particular need research-based vocabulary instruction that is embedded in all content classrooms:

- **Students with limited knowledge of English.** Academic English (English used in textbooks and printed material) is different from spoken or conversational English. This can present challenges for English language learners as they try to make sense of what they read, especially at the middle and high school levels.

- **Students who do not read outside of school.** As noted above, the amount of time spent reading and the amount read are highly correlated with vocabulary growth. Students who do not read outside of school have a great need for vocabulary instruction.

- **Students with learning disabilities.** Weaknesses in language processing skills at the phonological, orthographic, semantic, syntactic, and text levels caused by a learning disability can affect the ability to learn and remember new vocabulary words.

- **Students with weak decoding and/or fluency skills.** Weaknesses in phonics (decoding) and/or fluency skills prohibit students from reading grade-level content material and diminish the rich opportunity this material offers for encountering new, content-related words that can only be found in written English. Also, weak word analysis skills affects these students' ability to automatically recognize meaningful parts of words (i.e., roots, suffixes, prefixes), making it difficult to determine the meaning of unfamiliar words.

- **Students who enter school with limited vocabulary knowledge.** As noted above, differences in vocabulary knowledge upon entering school become magnified each year, resulting in high-performing 12th grade students knowing about four times as many words as low-performing 12th graders (Hart & Risley, 1995).

To overcome these obstacles, teachers need to incorporate the best kinds of vocabulary instruction into every aspect of their teaching, throughout the school day.

Effective Vocabulary Instruction: What the Research Says

What Works

In its analysis of the research on vocabulary instruction, the National Reading Panel (2000) found that there is no single best method for vocabulary instruction and that vocabulary should be taught both directly and indirectly. Direct instruction means focusing on specific words, such as previewing unfamiliar words prior to reading a selection, or selecting a set of subject-specific high frequency words to teach in-depth. However, it is impossible to directly teach all the words that students need to learn. Beck, McKeown, and Kucan (2002) estimate that students can be explicitly taught approximately 400 words per year in school. It is therefore necessary for teachers to identify specific words to teach in-depth.

Other examples of direct instruction include teaching word analysis skills, such as identifying roots and base words, suffixes, prefixes and teaching how to use context to determine word meaning. Vocabulary instruction should also include indirect approaches such as exposing students to many new words and having them read more. Indirect instruction also includes helping students develop an appreciation for words and experience enjoyment and satisfaction in their use (Baumann, et al., 2003).

In their review of the vocabulary instruction research, Pressley, Disney, and Anderson (2007) found that students comprehend more when they are taught vocabulary taken from text they are reading. However, teachers should not rely on a basal or core reading series as the sole source for providing vocabulary learning activities. Research has shown that vocabulary activities used in these materials (e.g., matching definitions) are often limited to simply providing definitions without opportunities for students to be engaged with word meanings enough to understand and remember them (Ryder & Graves, 1994; Bromley, 2002). Based on analyses of vocabulary lists from reading programs, it was found that many of these words are rare and occur at most once in a list of a million words taken from school texts (Lehr, et al., 2004). Instead, teachers need to provide what is called "rich vocabulary instruction" (Beck, et al., 1987; Beck, et al., 2002), which emphasizes long-term teaching of vocabulary that includes many encounters with the words and significant discussion and use of a word.

There is an extensive research base that suggests effective vocabulary instruction must be multicomponential. For example, Graves (2000) has advocated a four-part program that includes wide reading, teaching individual words, teaching word learning strategies, and fostering word consciousness. Pressley, Disney, & Anderson (2007) identify the following components as essential to an effective elementary or secondary classroom (p. 223 – 224):

- Immersing students in rich verbal interactions, especially meaningful and interesting conversations around worthwhile content experiences;

- Promoting extensive reading of worthwhile texts that are filled with mature vocabulary;

- Attending responsively to students' vocabulary needs (e.g., monitoring when they are struggling to identify a word);

- Finding ways to provide definitions to students of potentially unfamiliar words;

- Rich teaching of vocabulary words, involving extensive use of and experience with words over long periods of time;

- Teaching that the meaning of a word often can be inferred from the context clues; and

- Teaching the meaning of common word parts and providing practice in applying this knowledge to understanding unfamiliar words.

There is no best time or subject for teaching vocabulary. Given the huge number of words that need to be learned each year, a combination of direct and indirect instruction needs to take place throughout the school day in all subjects.

What Doesn't Work

For many years, the practice of having students look up words, copy definitions, and memorize those definitions was the main strategy used to teach vocabulary. However, there is a great deal of research showing that children cannot use conventional definitions to learn words (Scott & Nagy, 1997). Research conducted by Miller and Gildea (1987) challenged the long-held belief that asking students to look up the meanings of new words in the dictionary was the best way to teach vocabulary. They asked fifth and sixth grade students to read dictionary definitions for words they did not know and then write meaningful sentences containing the words. Even when the dictionary definition was accompanied by a model sentence, they found that students often were not able to show that they understood the word. This and similar research indicates that merely providing definitions, even with examples of words used in context, is an inadequate instructional practice. Yet this approach is often all that teachers use, especially during content classroom instruction.

Some schools and districts have adopted vocabulary programs that are usually taught only in English Language Arts classes. These programs typically provide weekly word lists that students are expected to learn through workbook activities and memorization of definitions. The words in these lists are unrelated to the content information or reading material they are using in their classes. Typically, students must learn the words for a quiz given at the end of the week. There is very little instruction provided during class time; students are expected to learn the word definitions for homework. Unfortunately, the use of this type of routine lulls teachers into thinking they are teaching vocabulary when in fact none of the research-based effective practices are being implemented. It is essential that teachers have access to information about what really works in terms of increasing student vocabulary knowledge.

Indirect Methods for Teaching Vocabulary

Wide Reading: The More You Read, the More Vocabulary You Learn

As noted above, the amount of student reading is highly correlated with vocabulary knowledge. One of the most important steps teachers can take to build students' vocabulary is to give them opportunities to read more (Anderson & Nagy, 1992; Stahl, 1999).

Multiple Exposure to Words

The growth of word knowledge is slow and incremental, requiring multiple exposures to words (Hirsch, 2003; Stahl, 2004). This does not mean simply repeating the word and a definition, but seeing the word in different contexts. How are words learned incrementally over multiple exposures? Every time we encounter a word in context, we remember something about the word. As we encounter a word repeatedly, more and more information accumulates about that word, and we move from having a vague notion of what it means to eventually being able to define and use it.

It is helpful for students to understand how they gradually learn words. Teachers should encourage students to actively construct links between new information and previously known information about a word.

The Importance of Background Knowledge and Teaching Related Words

Background knowledge refers to a student's experience and knowledge of the world. Research has established that readers' existing knowledge is critical for them to understand what they read (Anderson & Pearson, 1984). More than vocabulary is needed to understand most texts. It is possible for students to know all the words in a passage and still not make sense of it if they have no prior knowledge of the topic. To make constructive use of vocabulary, students need a threshold level of knowledge about the topic. This enables them to make sense of the word combinations and choose among multiple possible word meanings as they read (Hirsch, 2003). Therefore, words should be taught in meaningful contexts that convey the particular meaning relevant to the text being read.

People who know a great deal about a topic also know its vocabulary. Word meanings are not just unrelated bits of information, but are part of larger knowledge structures (Stahl, 1999). Schema theory was developed by the educational psychologist R. C. Anderson (1977, 1984). A schema is a mental plan that organizes knowledge to represent one's understanding of a particular topic. People use their schemata to organize current knowledge and provide a framework for future understanding. Schema theory has significant implications as it relates to comprehension and learning new information and words. When students can associate a new word or piece of information with an existing schema, they will learn it faster and remember it longer. Reading comprehension and vocabulary growth are best served by spending extended time reading texts on the same topic and discussing the ideas and new words in them to expand the students' schemata. This kind of immersion in a topic not only improves reading and develops vocabulary, but it also develops writing skills (Hirsch, 2003).

The Key Vocabulary Routine places a strong emphasis on teaching new vocabulary in relation to other new words and words that students already know. The Routine also emphasizes the value of vocabulary instruction that is embedded in content teaching in order to build the background knowledge related to new words. See Step 2 of *The Key Vocabulary Routine* for specific activities.

Direct Methods for Teaching Vocabulary

Provide Direct, Explicit Instruction for Specific Words

Although it is impossible to specifically teach all the new words students must learn, it is useful to provide direct instruction for some words. This includes previewing some unfamiliar vocabulary prior to reading so students will have some notion of what the words mean in order to make sense of the text. In addition, there are key vocabulary words that teachers can select to teach in-depth. It is estimated that students can be taught explicitly some 400 words per year in school (Beck et al., 2002). Teachers should remember that direct instruction of specific words is only one component of effective vocabulary instruction.

What words should teachers choose for direct instruction? Teachers should focus on words that are important to the text, useful to know in many situations, and uncommon in everyday language but recurring in books (Juel & Deffes, 2004).

Direct instruction of specific words should include teaching all aspects of the word, including the phonemes (sounds) in the word, the spelling of the word, its word parts (i.e., root and affixes), multiple meanings of the word, word concepts (such as word families, related words, and categories of words), and different associations (e.g., synonyms, antonyms).

Analyzing Word Structure: Teaching Word Parts

When students encounter unknown words they can sometimes use knowledge of word parts (roots, suffixes, prefixes) to help determine the meaning. This is especially true when reading content material because these texts often contain words that are derived from the same word parts.

Structural analysis of a word draws the student's attention to the individual units of meaning in the word, also known as *morphemes*. A *free morpheme* can stand alone (e.g., *cut*), while a *bound morpheme* needs to be attached to another morpheme (e.g., *ing, un*), and two free morphemes can combine to form a compound word (e.g., *airplane*) (Blachowicz & Fisher, 2004).

It is often assumed that the best person to teach word analysis skills is the English Language Arts teacher. However, content classrooms such as science and math often offer the greatest opportunity to encounter words with related parts. It is therefore important for all teachers to learn how to teach this essential skill.

Use of Context to Determine Word Meaning

Good readers often use context clues to determine the meanings of unfamiliar words, if these clues are available in the text. They can locate other words and phrases in a passage that give clues about what an unknown word means. However, many students do not intuitively apply this skill and require direct instruction in this area.

It is important to note that contexts vary in the degree to which they are helpful and the amount of information they provide a reader. In fact, sometimes the context can actually lead to a misunderstanding, referred to as a *misdirective* by Beck, McKeown, & Kucan (2002). Students must also be taught that even if the context provides clues to the meaning of the word, that meaning may be just one of multiple meanings (e.g., a *plane* in math is different from a *plane* in aeronautics).

Effective Use of a Dictionary

As noted above, research has shown that the use of dictionary definitions alone to teach new vocabulary does not work. That does not mean that students should not use dictionaries and other reference tools. Students must be taught explicitly how to transfer what they find in a dictionary entry into useful information. Students may be confused by multiple meanings for the same word or they might find that the wording in a dictionary entry is too complex and includes other unknown words.

Struggling readers and students with learning disabilities in particular have difficulty finding words in a dictionary. The process is slow and labored, often making the time it takes to look up a word frustrating and not worth the effort. Ideally, students should learn how to restate a definition in their own words. The key point to remember about using a dictionary is that research supports combining both the definitions of new words with the context in which the words are used.

Fostering Word Consciousness

Vocabulary instruction is most effective when students are actively involved in the process of learning the words. Anderson and Nagy (1992) define word consciousness as having both a cognitive and an affective stance towards words, characterized by having awareness about words, a motivation to learn words, and an interest in words. Graves (2006) notes that students who are word conscious are aware of the words around them, appreciate the power of words, and understand why certain words are used instead of others. Graves identifies two reasons why it is important for teachers to promote word consciousness:

1. For students of all ages, motivation and affect are as important to learning as cognition. Word consciousness should therefore be the motivational and affective component of a multifaceted vocabulary program.

2. The lack of vocabulary is a key factor underlying school failure for disadvantaged students. Creating students' interest and engagement with words is vital to helping these students develop strong vocabularies.

Examples of activities that can be used to foster word consciousness include:

- Teaching metalinguistic awareness (i.e., the ability to reflect on and manipulate words and parts of words) (Scott and Nagy, 2004)

- Talking about language use by good authors (Scott and Nagy, 2004)

- Creating a word-rich environment, including word play games such as word riddles, card games, anagrams, and word challenges (Blachowicz and Fisher, 2004b)

Activities for developing word consciousness do not necessarily have to be specifically planned. Teachers need to take word consciousness into account coincidentally throughout the day (Scott and Nagy, 2004).

Connecting the Research to The Key Vocabulary Routine

The Key Vocabulary Routine is a model for embedding direct and indirect instruction in content classroom instruction. The instructional practices are organized into a common set of foundational activities that can be used with any subject matter. Every activity in the Routine is research-based as presented in this chapter.

Beck, McKeown, and Kucan (2002) suggest that vocabulary instruction in middle and high schools should be more "rooted to text and dealt with in a way that both teaches the words and brings enriched understanding to the text" (p. 85). *The Key Vocabulary Routine* offers a consistent approach for teaching vocabulary as students move from grade to grade and from teacher to teacher, and connects the research to practice.

Full passage from Activity 2

Just then the <u>stern</u> line came <u>taut</u> under his foot, where he had kept a <u>loop</u> of the line, and he dropped his <u>oars</u> and felt the <u>weight</u> of the small <u>tuna's</u> <u>shivering</u> pull as he held the line <u>firm</u> and <u>commenced</u> to <u>haul</u> it in. The <u>shivering</u> <u>increased</u> as he pulled in and he could see the blue back of the fish in the <u>water</u> and the <u>gold</u> of his sides before he <u>swung</u> him over the side and into the boat. He <u>lay</u> in the <u>stern</u> in the sun, <u>compact</u> and bullet shaped, his big <u>unintelligent</u> eyes <u>staring</u> as he thumped his life out against the <u>planking</u> of the boat with the quick <u>shivering</u> <u>strokes</u> of his neat, fast-moving tail.

From: Ernest Hemingway, *The Old Man and The Sea*

NOTES:

Part 2

The Five Steps in
The Key Vocabulary Routine

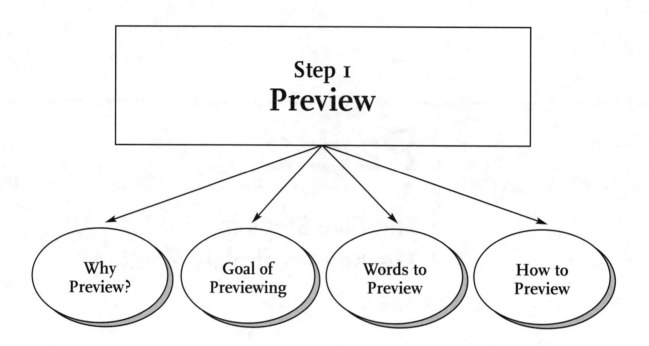

Step 1: Preview for Difficult Vocabulary

Why Preview Vocabulary?

Studies have shown that pre-teaching vocabulary can improve comprehension (Laflamme, 1997; Billmeyer & Barton, 1998). Existing background knowledge is a critical component for comprehension, and word meanings are part of larger knowledge structures, or schema about a topic. Knowing the vocabulary words associated with a given topic enables students to connect their background knowledge to what they are listening to or reading. In order to fully comprehend while reading, a person must be familiar with at least 90 percent of the words in the text (Hirsch, 2003). This connection between background knowledge and vocabulary has several implications for teaching:

- Preview words before reading to activate and provide background knowledge, as well as address incorrect prior knowledge.

- Provide basic knowledge about unknown words before reading so students can comprehend.

- Teach words in relation to other known words and existing schema about a topic.

The Goal of Previewing

Previewing vocabulary before reading works as a comprehension strategy. The goal of previewing is to:

- Activate prior knowledge;

- Clear up student misconceptions about word meaning;

- Clarify the meaning of known words in relation to the current context, especially for words with multiple meanings; and

- Provide some initial familiarity with unknown words so students can make sense of the text.

There may be many words or phrases that are unfamiliar to students, but it is not worth spending time teaching all these words. Previewing is about attaching some meaning to new words rather than deeply learning these words. It is important to provide deep, direct instruction for certain key words, but previewing before reading is not the best time to do this. The goal of previewing is to provide students with just enough knowledge about those words that are central to the meaning of what they will read. Graves (2006) notes:

> In one case you may just want to introduce the word so the students won't stumble over it when they see it in an upcoming passage. In another, you will want to give students deep, rich and lasting meaning for a word. (p. 60)

Marzano (2004) makes a similar point:

> ... words do not have to be known at a deep level to be useful to an individual. In fact, when we encounter a word, we initially access the surface-level characteristics first... Complete word knowledge might not be necessary for all words that students learn. For some terms, the target of instruction might be that students have an accurate, albeit incomplete, understanding that would form the foundation on which students might build a deeper understanding through repeated interactions with the words (pp. 107-108).

The point is to not spend a significant amount of time pre-teaching in-depth all of the words that may be unfamiliar to students. Many teachers, unfortunately, use previewing as their main way to teach vocabulary and believe they need to deeply teach every word on a previewing list. There are just too many unknown words that will come up in daily reading to be able to teach them all.

What Words Should Be Previewed?

Teachers should begin by reading the material to identify words that may be unfamiliar to students but essential to understanding the text. These are the words that should be previewed. Choosing which words to preview will depend on the students in the class, including issues like grade level, vocabulary and background knowledge, and English proficiency. For students in the same grade level reading the same passage, words for previewing may be different from school to school, and even from classroom to classroom. Teachers must, therefore, use common sense, sensitivity, and knowledge about their students to determine which words to preview. Here are some suggestions to help you determine which words to preview:

- Choose words that are necessary to understand the text.

- Choose words that are essential to understanding the major concepts in the content lesson or unit of study.

- Choose words that are unfamiliar specialized academic words (e.g., metamorphosis, quadrilateral, oligarchy), and non-specialized academic words (e.g., analyze, relationship, synthesize) that are essential to comprehending the topic of the reading.

- Choose words that are unfamiliar to most of the students.

- Include problematic phrases or figurative language.

- Choose words that have unfamiliar multiple meanings.

- Consider leaving out words that are clearly defined within the context or that students can make sense of given clues in the text.

- Do not rely on the textbook to identify words for previewing.

Another good resource for determining which words to preview is the students themselves. Ask them to skim the passage and make a list of words they do not know. When students do this activity in small, cooperative groups, each group generates a list, and the teacher generates a master previewing list based on the input from the groups.

Activity 1: Generate a Sample Preview List

Directions: Using a reading selection from your classroom, create a previewing list of at least 20 words and phrases. Remember, you can include any words or phrases that may affect comprehension, not just words that you will teach in-depth.

1. appreciate
2. roll call
3. wilted
4. scarcely
5. icing
6. envious
7. jealous
8. jaundice
9. trifle
10. spiffy
11.
12.
13.
14.
15.
16.
17.
18.

19. _____

20. _____

21. _____

22. _____

23. _____

24. _____

25. _____

How Should Words be Previewed?

For some teachers, the primary way to preview words is to instruct students to look up words in a dictionary or glossary and memorize the definitions. However, this approach does not transfer knowledge about the word into useful ownership by the student, and it often does not provide enough understanding to help make sense of the reading. Frequently, dictionary definitions are confusing, and they do not connect the meaning of the word to the subject matter or the reading context. It is also time consuming.

The best way to preview words is to spend a limited amount of time providing a basic understanding about the words. There may be some words from a previewing list that should be selected to teach in greater depth, but not at this point. Here are some ways to effectively preview vocabulary:

- **Provide synonyms and antonyms:** Provide words to students that are related to the preview word, either similar in meaning or opposite in meaning. A thesaurus can be helpful for this.

- **Use everyday language to explain the words:** Provide user-friendly definitions, especially as the meaning relates to the context of the reading. Based on many years of research and work with teachers on vocabulary instruction, Beck and McKeown (2007) have developed an approach to teaching words that they call "rich" instruction. This approach uses everyday language to explain the meanings of words. Rich instruction suggests the following be used during previewing:

  - Introduce words through explanations in everyday connected language rather than dictionary definitions
  - Provide several contexts in which the word can be used
  - Provide examples, situations, and questions that are interesting
  - Encourage students to interact with the word right away by asking them to relate to and talk about the word in some way

- **Use discussion:** Discussion has been found to be an effective way to learn unfamiliar words, and several vocabulary specialists recommend discussion as a way to preview new words before reading (McKeown & Beck, 1988; Carlisle and Katz, 2005). When teachers present unfamiliar words in context and ask students to offer possible meanings, the ensuing discussion improves students' understanding of words. A simple way to review words on a previewing list is for the teacher to facilitate a whole class discussion about the words or to monitor small collaborative group discussions.

- **Use collaborative, small groups:** Encourage students to work collaboratively to make connections between the words and to check each other's understanding of the words.

- **Use a Word Knowledge Checklist:** The growth of word knowledge is slow and incremental, requiring multiple exposures to words. Often, students may not know the full meaning of a word or be able to produce a definition, yet they still may have enough familiarity with a word to be able to comprehend while reading. Word Knowledge Checklists can be used to help students make a connection to words even if they do not completely know the word. These checklists also reinforce that words are learned incrementally over time and that students do not need deep knowledge of every word to comprehend while reading. See Figure A below for an example.

The best way to use a Word Knowledge Checklist is to have students work on them in small collaborative groups. This results in rich discussion of the words and other related words. The opportunity to engage with peers builds confidence and interest for learning new words. Another way to make students aware of their knowledge is to put words on cards and ask students to put the word cards into piles based on the checklist headings. This physical manipulation of vocabulary can be motivating for some students.

Figure A

Word Knowledge Checklist

Word	Know it well, can explain it, use it	Know something about it, can relate it to a situation	Have seen or heard the word	Do not know the word

Beck, McKeown, & Kucan, 2002

[handwritten note in left margin: leave a few blank lines on bottom for students to fill in.]

Resource Tip: *Word Web* (www.wordwebonline.com) is a free dictionary and thesaurus software program that can be accessed online and can also be downloaded onto a computer desktop to be used without the Internet. When a vocabulary word or phrase, including figurative language such as *raining cats and dogs,* is entered into the search feature, definitions, synonyms, and antonyms are provided. For some words, direct links to online encyclopedia entries are also provided. It is a simple tool for providing instant access to previewing information about words.

Activity 2: Practice Previewing

Part 1

Directions: Use the Word Knowledge Checklist to rate your knowledge of these words before you read the sample research passage.

Word	Know it well, can explain it use it	Know something about it, can relate it to a situation	Have seen or heard the word	Do not know the word
encounter	✓			
context	✓			
phonologically	✓			
orthographically			✓	
lexical			✓	
inferential	✓			
initiate	✓			
cues	✓			
vague	✓			
incidental	✓			
contextual clues	✓			
morphological		✓		
acquire		✓		

Beck, McKeown, & Kucan, 2002

[handwritten margin notes: "Study of correct spelling", "long associated with someone or something", "parts of a word", "Study of the smallest meaning of a word"]

Part 2

Directions: Work in small groups and discuss the meaning of each word. Then answer the questions.

Did the discussion clarify or broaden your understanding of any of the words? Explain.

_____

_____

_____

_____

_____

For words about which you were unsure, did the discussion help build enough background knowledge so you will not "stumble" over the words that were unknown to you?

_____

_____

_____

_____

_____

What can the instructor do to provide you with enough knowledge about the unfamiliar words so you can successfully read the passage?

_____

_____

_____

_____

_____

Part 3

Directions: Read the sample research passage below and answer the questions.

"For children, as well as adults, learning an unfamiliar word begins when it is encountered in an oral or written language context and when understanding of that word matters to the listener or reader. If a word is encoded phonologically (and, in written contexts, orthographically) but no lexical representation is available, an inferential process is initiated such that cues from the immediate context of the new word are used to assign some sort of meaning, if only a vague association with the topic. This process is called *incidental word learning*. It is the primary way that people, regardless of age, learn new words. Incidental word learning, which depends on both contextual clues and morphological analysis, is the primary means through which students acquire new vocabulary."

Adapted from: Carlisle, J.F. (2007). Fostering morphological processing, vocabulary development, and reading comprehension. In R.K. Wagner, A.E. Muse, & K.R. Tannenbaum (Eds.). *Vocabulary acquisition: Implications for reading comprehension*. New York: The Guilford Press.

Was your comprehension of the passage improved because words were previewed?

_____

Are there any other words you or your peers may be unsure of that should be added to the previewing list?

_____

_____

_____

_____

Part 4

Directions: Review the Word Knowledge Checklist and determine if you can now change the rating for any of the words.

Activity 3: Practice Planning

Directions: Use the suggestions in this chapter to develop a previewing lesson plan for a previewing list. The following template can be used for this purpose.

Class period: _____

Date(s) covered: _____

Reading Selection: _____

Words to Preview

1. _____   14. _____
2. _____   15. _____
3. _____   16. _____
4. _____   17. _____
5. _____   18. _____
6. _____   19. _____
7. _____   20. _____
8. _____   21. _____
9. _____   22. _____
10. _____   23. _____
11. _____   24. _____
12. _____   25. _____
13. _____

Activities I will use to provide familiarity with these words and to make connections to existing student background knowledge:

_____

_____

_____

_____

_____

_____

_____

Step 1 Summary

The goal of previewing is to provide some familiarity and background knowledge for words or phrases that students may not know so their reading comprehension will not be impaired by the lack of this knowledge. The goal is not to teach all of the previewing words in-depth. Previewing also helps to activate and build background knowledge about the topic of the reading. A previewing activity should be done in the classroom and take a limited amount of time. Students should not be asked to look up and copy definitions, or use the words in sentences for homework. Teachers should select the words for previewing based on the specific needs of the students, and students can also participate in selecting troublesome words.

NOTES:

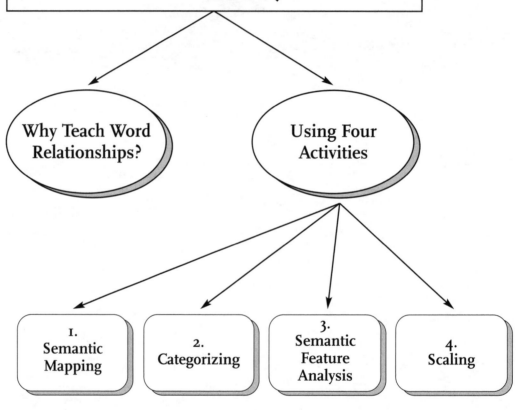

Step 2
Activities to Connect Vocabulary

Why Teach Word Relationships?

Using Four Activities

1. Semantic Mapping

2. Categorizing

3. Semantic Feature Analysis

4. Scaling

Step 2: Use Activities to Connect Vocabulary

Step 2 of *The Key Vocabulary Routine* involves making connections between new words and other related words. It is helpful for students to learn a new content word by associating it with other related words from the same content area. The related words can be words students already know or new words. There are four activities that can be used to teach the relationship between words: **Semantic Mapping, Categorizing, Semantic Feature Analysis,** and **Scaling.**

Why Teaching Words in Relationship to Other Words is Helpful

Knowledge helps you remember new information, and people who know a great deal about a topic also know its vocabulary. One critical finding from recent research is that word learning takes place most efficiently when the reader or listener already understands the context well. In fact, we learn words up to four times faster in a familiar context than in an unfamiliar one (Landauer & Dumais, 1997; Hirsch, 2006). Vocabulary instruction that compares and contrasts word meanings and that activates prior knowledge not only helps students learn new words, but has also been shown to improve comprehension of the reading selection (Graves, 2006). Therefore, an important goal of instruction in any subject area should be to help students acquire the vocabulary associated with the content while learning the content and to make connections between known and unknown words.

Another reason to teach new words in relation to other words is to provide information that is unique to how that word is being used in context. Many words have multiple meanings and different connotations depending on the subject area. They can also be different parts of speech. For example, the words *development* and *root* have multiple meanings and different content area connotations (see the multiple meanings for these words at the end of this chapter). When associations can be made to other words, especially words that students already know, students will acquire a better understanding of how a new word is being used in a specific text or related classroom discussion.

Using the Four Activities

There are four activities that can be used in *The Key Vocabulary Routine* to teach words in relation to other words: **Semantic Mapping, Categorizing, Semantic Feature Analysis** and **Scaling.** Of these, the best known and most widely researched are Semantic Mapping and Semantic Feature Analysis. All four activities have the following in common:

- They make connections between new words and known words.

- They make connections between background knowledge about concepts and words associated with the concepts.

- They offer opportunities for rich discussion about words.

- They push students to go beyond simply learning definitions to actively thinking about the connections between word meanings and how words are similar and different.

Students are better able to learn unfamiliar words when they are actively involved in meaning making. Using semantic mapping, categorizing, semantic feature analysis, or scaling as a whole class or in small collaborative groups is an excellent way to generate rich discussion. As students engage in these activities, opportunities arise for them to hear and discuss a number of related words that may not even be in the text or part of the teacher's chosen word list. As they discuss the subtleties of word meanings and relate them to the text they are reading, they will activate and create background knowledge.

These activities can be used before, during, or after students read or are presented with content information in class. They can be used with words from a previewing list or applied to specific words which will be taught in-depth. Teachers are not expected to use all four activities with every set of vocabulary words. They can decide to selectively use those activities that work best for the words they are teaching. It is almost always possible to identify a key word to do a Semantic Mapping Activity, but Semantic Feature Analysis and Scaling are not always easily applied to some word lists. Categorizing works for most, but not all, word lists.

Finally, in order to effectively use these activities, teachers need to spend time planning activities, scaffolding lessons, and differentiating instruction depending on the background knowledge of the students.

1. Semantic Mapping

Semantic mapping (Heimlich & Pittelman, 1986) is a well-researched visual tool that helps readers draw on background knowledge of a topic and see connections between ideas and words related to that topic. It is also highly interactive. A semantic map is usually constructed prior to reading, but can be revisited after reading. Figure A highlights the steps for a semantic mapping activity.

Figure A

Semantic Mapping

When to use

- Can be used before or after reading

Benefits

- Helps students make connections between known and unknown words

- Helps students activate background knowledge

- Provides an opportunity for rich discussion

How it is done

- Select a key concept word and place it in the middle of the board

- Conduct a group brainstorm; write down student-generated words relating to the concept word

- Students make connections between words and generate meaningful categories

- Reorganize words into groups by category

Variations

- The teacher provides a word bank, categories, or clues to support brainstorming

- Students generate additional words after categories are established

- Students generate additional words after reading or further class instruction

---

To generate a semantic map, the teacher chooses a key concept word that is central to the topic covered in the reading or classroom lesson and writes this word in the center of a page or on the board. Students are then asked to brainstorm as many words as they know associated with the key word. This brainstorming is best done as a whole class or in cooperative groups. The teacher or a student scribe writes the words generated on the board. Figure B is an example of an initial brainstorm map.

Figure B

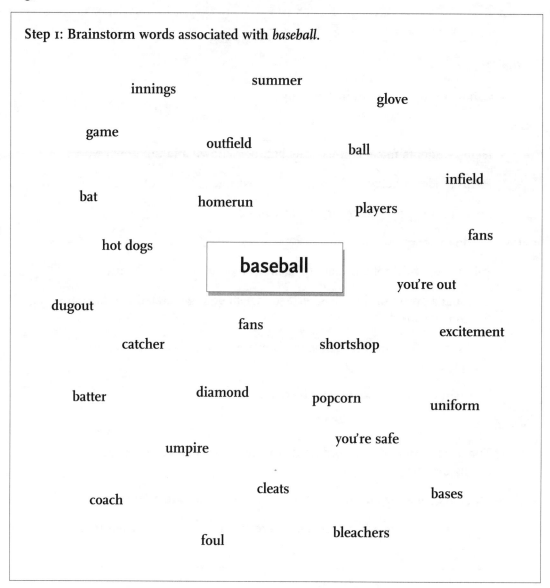

Step 1: Brainstorm words associated with *baseball*.

innings • summer • glove • game • outfield • ball • infield • bat • homerun • players • fans • hot dogs • **baseball** • you're out • dugout • fans • excitement • catcher • shortshop • batter • diamond • popcorn • uniform • umpire • you're safe • coach • cleats • bases • foul • bleachers

Once a significant number of words have been generated, students make connections between the words, group them, and assign categories for these groupings. Figure C is an example of the words organized into categories.

Figure C

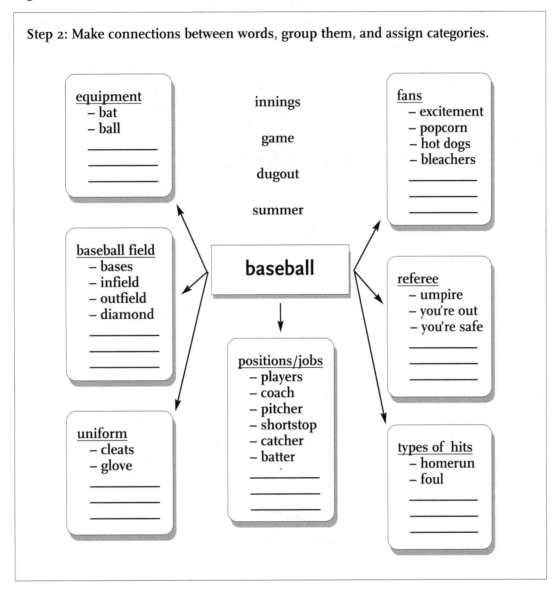

Step 2: Make connections between words, group them, and assign categories.

<u>equipment</u>
 – bat
 – ball
 _____
 _____
 _____

innings

game

dugout

summer

<u>fans</u>
 – excitement
 – popcorn
 – hot dogs
 – bleachers
 _____
 _____
 _____

<u>baseball field</u>
 – bases
 – infield
 – outfield
 – diamond
 _____
 _____
 _____

baseball

<u>referee</u>
 – umpire
 – you're out
 – you're safe
 _____
 _____
 _____

<u>uniform</u>
 – cleats
 – glove
 _____
 _____
 _____

<u>positions/jobs</u>
 – players
 – coach
 – pitcher
 – shortstop
 – catcher
 – batter
 _____
 _____
 _____

<u>types of hits</u>
 – homerun
 – foul
 _____
 _____
 _____
 _____

Sometimes one of the words becomes a category (e.g., *uniform*), and sometimes the word for the category needs to be generated (e.g., *referee, equipment*). Once the categories are identified, students can add more words to each category. Sometimes there will be words that cannot be grouped into a category (e.g., *innings, game, summer, dugout*).

Sometimes a new concept word will be so foreign to students that they are unable to generate their own words. For example, the background experience for students growing up in a city may not be sufficient to brainstorm many words related to the word *harvest*. When this happens, teachers should provide some background knowledge to get the brainstorming started.

Teachers can scaffold a semantic mapping activity by providing a word bank to get students going, by providing topic words or categories before students brainstorm, or by providing clues during the brainstorm. Also, once students have finished reading or at the end of instruction about the topic, they can go back to the semantic map and add more words.

Discussion should be encouraged throughout a semantic mapping activity. By listening and sharing, students learn new words and clarify their knowledge about words they already know. Out of the four activities in Step 2 of *The Key Vocabulary Routine*, semantic mapping best connects vocabulary words to background content knowledge.

Activity 1: Practice Generating a Semantic Map

Part 1

Directions: Complete a brainstorm mapping activity for the word humor.

humor

Part 2

Directions: Make connections between the words and generate meaningful categories. You may also add new words.

humor

Part 3

Directions: Answer the questions.

Did some of the words that were brainstormed become category words?

_____

_____

Were there words that could not be grouped with other words to form a category?

_____

_____

Once the categories were generated, were you able to brainstorm additional words?

_____

_____

Activity 2: Practice Planning

Directions: Identify a key concept word from the list you generated in the previewing activity or from a unit of study you teach. Use this word to develop a semantic mapping activity. Use the space below for the brainstorming map and the categories, or use a separate piece of paper.

Technology Tip: If a Smart Board or LCD projector and computer are available for class instruction, teachers can use mapping software such as Inspiration (www.inspiration.com) or Smart Ideas (www2.smarttech.com/st/en-US/Products/SMART+Ideas/) to help generate a semantic map. Software of this type enables the user to type in words while brainstorming, and then easily move the words around on the page during the categorizing stage of the activity.

2. Categorizing

Categorizing involves grouping, or *chunking*, words into categories. Figure D highlights the steps for a categorizing activity.

Figure D

Categorizing

When to use

- Used after reading; when students have some knowledge of the words it can be used before or during reading

- Can be used with a list of preview words or words selected for in-depth instruction

Benefits

- Helps students make connections between known and unknown words.

- Provides an opportunity for rich discussion

How it is done

- Provide students with a list of words

- Students make connections between words and generate meaningful categories

- Students list words under categories

Variations

- The teacher provides the categories

- Students generate additional words to add to the category words

---

To generate a categorizing activity, the teacher creates a list of words. The teacher can provide the categories or the students can be asked to determine the categories. Some knowledge of the words is necessary in order to categorize, so it is best to do this activity after words have been previewed or after students have read a passage containing the words. Teachers should not expect students to categorize words they do not know for homework.

For the words in Figure E, two obvious categories might be *fruits* (apple, banana, grape, orange, pear) and *vegetables* (asparagus, broccoli, spinach, string bean). With any given list of words, there may be multiple options for categories. For example, *green food* (apple, asparagus, broccoli, grape, pear, spinach, string bean) or *round food* (apple, donut, grape, orange). Sometimes there may be words that do not fit into any logical category, such as *chocolate*. Sometimes words can fall under more than one category (*apple* fits under *fruit*, *round food*, and *green food*).

Another option for categorizing is to ask students to generate additional words associated with the topic that can be added to the categories. Using Figure E as an example, students might add *carrot* to the vegetable list, or *plum* to the fruit list. This is especially helpful for making connections between known and unknown words.

Figure E

Word List

apple	asparagus	banana
broccoli	donut	grape
orange	pear	spinach
string bean	chocolate	

Memory of new information is enhanced when the words are connected to an existing schema of knowledge. The more specific the categories can be, the stronger the memory will be.

Not all lists of words lend themselves to categorizing. Sometimes there are only a few words that can be grouped into a category. Word lists that are generated from subject reading such as history, science, or math tend to lend themselves to categorizing, while it might be more difficult to find connections between words selected from literature.

It is important to note that there are no right or wrong answers when categorizing words. In fact, sometimes students generate some very interesting categories, providing insight into their thinking about the topic in general and the words associated with that topic.

It should also be noted that categorizing is an excellent activity for teaching and practicing main idea skills, an essential building block for teaching other comprehension strategies such as note taking and summarizing. Categorizing and other strategy activities such as taking two-column notes, summarizing, and generating questions are addressed in *The Key Comprehension Routine,* another program published by Keys to Literacy that embeds research-based comprehension strategies in content literacy instruction.

Activity 3: Practice Categorizing

Directions: Review the list of words related to Egypt and generate possible categories. Then answer the questions.

Words

Amulet: charm worn to bring good luck

Anubis: god of the afterlife

Book of the Dead: a collection of spells/prayers to help with the passage to the afterlife

Canopic jars: containers for the internal organs of an embalmed body

Cartouche: oval shape surrounding an inscription of a royal name

---

Cataracts: steep rapids in a river
Delta: where the water leaves the river and enters the sea
Giza: the place where the pyramids were built
Hatshepsut: first female ruler of the New Kingdom of Egypt
Imhoptep: the architect who designed the first pyramid for King Zoser
Inundation: annual flooding of the Nile
Kush: country to the south of Egypt
Luxor: the place of royal cemeteries
Mastaba: rectangular shaped tomb with sloping sides and a flat top
Menes: king who first unified upper and lower Egypt
Natron: a mineral/salt used in mummification
Obelisk: a tall and thin four-sided stone pillar
Papyrus: water reed used for making paper
Pharaoh: title for the rulers of Egypt
Ra: the first, most important Egyptian god
Red Sea: sea that borders Egypt on the east
Sarcophagus: a stone coffin
Scarab: an amulet in the form of a beetle
Scribes: professional writers or record keepers
Shroud: a cloth in which a dead body is wrapped
Sphinx: a statue with the head of a human and the body of a lion
Tributary: a small river that feeds into the Nile

Options for Categories

1. _____

2. _____

3. _____

4. _____

Was there disagreement about possible categories or whether a word belonged under a certain category? If so, how did the discussion help you to think more closely about the subtleties and importance of context for any of the words?

_____

_____

Can you add more words to the categories related to the topic?

_____

_____

What other interesting words came up during group discussion?

_____

_____

Activity 4: Practice Planning

Directions: Use the list of words you generated in the previewing activity or identify words from a unit of study you teach to develop a categorizing activity.

<u>Words</u>

_____   _____   _____

_____   _____   _____

_____   _____   _____

_____   _____   _____

_____   _____   _____

_____   _____   _____

Options for Categories

1. _____

2. _____

3. _____

4. _____

3. Semantic Feature Analysis

Semantic feature analysis (Baldwin et al., 1981; Johnson & Pearson, 1984) is another well-researched activity that helps students recognize similarities and differences between related words. A relational matrix, or grid, is used to show how related words are alike and different. When a semantic feature matrix is completed, it provides a good overall view of concept features. Figure F highlights the steps for a semantic feature analysis activity.

Figure F

Semantic Feature Analysis

When to use

- Used after reading; when students have some knowledge of the words, it can be used before or during reading

- Can be used with a list of preview words or words selected for in-depth instruction

Benefits

- Helps students make connections between known and unknown words

- Helps students recognize similarities and differences between related words

- Provides an opportunity for rich discussion

How it is done

- Present students with a grid that contains a set of related words on one axis and a list of features on the other axis

- Students identify the relationship between each word and feature by putting a plus (+) or minus (-) sign in the corresponding box on the grid

Variations

- Students add words or features to the grid

To generate a semantic feature analysis matrix, the teacher selects a list of related vocabulary words and places them along the left column or the top row of a grid. Knowledge of at least some of the words is necessary in order to begin, so it is best to do this activity after words have been previewed or after students have read a passage containing the words. Down or across the opposing axis of the grid, the teacher supplies features that highlight how these words might be similar and different. To complete the grid, students consider each word and determine if each feature applies to the word. A plus sign (+) is placed in the corresponding block on the grid if the feature is associated with the word, and a minus sign (-) is placed if it is not. If students are not sure, a question mark (?) can be placed in the block.

Sometimes, depending on the context, both a plus or minus sign can be given. There is often no absolutely correct answer, but through discussion and disagreement about whether a feature is applicable or not, a deeper understanding of the word meanings develops. Unique vocabulary words may be in the word axis or the feature axis. An extension of the activity is to have students generate additional related terms for the vocabulary axis, or to generate additional features.

Figure G contains three examples of a semantic feature analysis matrix.

Figure G

Math Example

Words	Features					
	2 dimensional	3 dimensional	contains equal angles	has curves	has straight lines	has a flat surface
line	–	–	–	–	+	+
square	+	–	+	–	+	+
cube	–	+	+	–	+	+
rectangle	+	–	+	–	+	+
circle	+	–	–	+	–	+
ball	–	+	–	+	–	–
prism	–	+	+/–	–	+	+
cylinder	–	+	–	+	–	+
equilateral triangle	+	–	+	–	+	+
isosceles triangle	+	–	–	–	+	+
pyramid	–	+	+	–	–	+

Literature Example: Characters from *Johnny Tremain*

Personality Traits	Characters									
	Johnny Tremain	Mr. Lapham	Dove	Cilla	John Hancock	Paul Revere	Rob	Lavinia Lyte	Mr. Lyte	General Gage
rebellious	+	−	−	+	+	+	+	−	−	−
indecisive	−	−	+	−	−	−	−	+	−	−
hostile	−	−	−	−	−	−	−	−	+	+
courageous	+	+	−	−	+	+	+	−	−	+
ambitious	+	+	−	−	+	+	+	−	−	+
sympathetic	+	+	−	+	+	+	−	+	−	−
suspicious	+	−	+	+	+	+	+	−	+	+
honest	+	+	−	+	+	+	+	+	−	−
ostentatious	−	−	−	−	−	−	−	+	+	−
affluent	−	−	−	−	+	+	−	+	+	−
industrious	+	+	−	+	+	+	+	−	−	+
competitive	+	−	−	−	+	+	+	−	+	+
loyal	+	+	+	+	+	+	+	−	−	−

From: *Johnny Tremain* by Esther Forbes, 1960. Boston: Houghton Mifflin.

History Example

Features	Forms of Government										
	anarchy	aristocracy	communist state	confederation	democracy	federation	monarchy	oligarchy	republic	theocracy	totalitarianism
Ruled by one party	−	−	+	−	−	−	+	−	−	+	+
Ruled by a single leader	−	−	−	−	−	−	+	−	−	+/−	+
Has multiple rulers	−	+	+	+	+	+	−	+	+	+/−	−
Ruler gains power through heredity	−	−	−	−	−	−	+	−	−	−	−
Ruler(s) have power for life	−	−	−	−	−	−	+	−	−	−	+/−
Citizens have impact on government	+	−	+	+/−	+	+/−	−	+/−	+	−	−
Has centrally planned economies	−	+/−	+	+	−	+/−	+	+/−	−	+	+
Union consisting of several states	−	−	−	−	+/−	+	−	−	−	−	−
State regulates public and private life	−	+	+	−	−	−	+	+/−	−	+	+
God or deity is recognized as the state's ruler	−	−	−	+/−	−	−	+/−	−	−	+	−
Has a free electoral system	−	−	−	+/−	+	+/−	−	−	+	−	−

Activity 5: Practice Semantic Feature Analysis

Directions: Complete the semantic feature analysis grid below in a small group. Then answer and discuss the questions.

	Narrow	Wide	Paved	Unpaved	For walking	For driving
path	✓	✓	✓	✓	✓	
trail	✓			✓	✓	
road	✓	✓	✓	✓	✓	✓
lane	✓		✓	✓	✓	✓
boulevard		✓	✓		✓	✓
freeway		✓	✓			✓
turnpike		✓	✓			✓

From: Graves, M.F. (2006). *The vocabulary book*. New York: Teachers College Press.

Was there disagreement about features for any of the words? If so, did the discussion that ensued cause you to think more closely about the complexity of meaning and the importance of context for any of the words?

_____

_____

Can you add any words to the left column or features along the top row?

_____

_____

What other interesting words came up during group discussion?

_____

Activity 6: Practice Planning

Directions: Identify words from the list you generated in the previewing activity or from a unit of study you teach that lend themselves to a semantic feature analysis activity.

Words	Features				

4. Scaling

Scaling (Moats, 2005), also described as "linear arrays" (Allen, 1999), is an activity that focuses on synonyms and antonyms. Based on a vocabulary word or pair of opposite words, a series of related words are generated along a continuum or scale. Figure H highlights the steps for a scaling activity.

Figure H

Scaling

When to use

- Can be used with one or more words from a list of previewing words or words selected for in-depth instruction

Benefits

- Helps students make connections between known and unknown words

- Provides an opportunity for rich discussion

How it is done

- Choose one word from a word list and generate an opposite of the word, or choose a pair of opposite words from a word list

- Place the words on opposite ends of a line, leaving room between the words and at each end of the scale

- Students generate words and place them along the continuum

Variations

- The teacher provides the words and students determine where they should be placed on the scale

---

To generate a scaling activity, the teacher chooses a key vocabulary word and identifies an antonym (opposite) for that word. The teacher places the pair of words on either end of a line, leaving room between the words and at each end of the line to add words. Students are asked to generate related words and place them along the scale based on their relationship to the original pair of words. The words may be placed anywhere between the two words, or beyond the words on each end of the scale. Sometimes a word list will contain a pair of opposite words that can be used for each end of the scale, as well as other words that can be placed on the scale.

Scaling is similar to semantic mapping because students brainstorm and generate many of their own words. Scaling can be scaffolded by providing a list of related words and then asking the students to determine where along the continuum the words should be placed.

Figure I has two examples of a scaling activity. The first uses several words from a content word list about the Middle Ages. This scale is based on social position and power. *Serf* and *King* were chosen as the opposites on the scale. *Page, squire, knight,* and *jester* were from the word list, but students added *slave, merchant, priest, noble, bishop,* and *prince*. The second example is based on one word that a teacher decided to teach in-depth: *deride*. Students generated all of the other words along the scale.

Figure I

Example 1

<u>Word List: Middle Ages</u>
jester: a funny performer who provides entertainment to the king
king: ruler of a kingdom
knight: fighter from a noble family
page: a boy in training to be a knight
serf: a peasant who works the land owned by someone else
squire: assistant to a knight

King (opposite word)
Prince
Jester
Bishop
Knight
Squire
Page
Noble
Priest
Merchant
Serf (opposite word)
slave

Example 2

<u>Target Word:</u> *deride*

ridicule
deride (target word)
be rude
ignore
disregard
not notice
recognize
be nice
like
compliment
flatter
adore
worship

Scaling does not work for all vocabulary words, only for those that have clear opposites and for which a variety of synonyms and related words can be generated. As with the other activities in Step 2, scaling provides an excellent opportunity for rich discussion.

Activity 7: Practice Scaling

Directions: Work in a small group to complete this scale. Then answer the questions.

```
↑   _____
    _____
        histrionic
    _____
    _____
    _____
    _____
    _____
    _____
    _____
    _____
    _____
    _____
    _____
    _____
    _____
        emotionless
    _____
↓   _____
```

Were any synonyms generated that you thought should be placed at the same level on the scale?

_____

_____

Was there disagreement about where a word should be placed along the scale? If so, how did the discussion cause you to think more closely about the complexity of meaning and the importance of context for the word?

_____

_____

What other interesting words came up during group discussion?

_____

_____

Activity 8: Practice Planning

Directions: Choose a word or words from the list of words you generated in the previewing activity or from a unit of study you teach to develop a scaling activity.

Step 2 Summary

Semantic Mapping, Categorizing, Semantic Feature Analysis, and Scaling are four activities for learning new words by associating them with related words. These activities help students make connections between background knowledge about concepts and words associated with those concepts. They also offer opportunities for rich discussion about words.

Multiple Meanings for the Words *development* and *root*

development
1. Act of improving by expanding or enlarging or refining *"He congratulated them on their development of a plan to meet the emergency.";* *"They funded research and development."*

2. A process in which something passes by degrees to a different stage (especially a more advanced or mature stage)
   "The development of his ideas took many years.";
   "the slow development of her skill as a writer."
   —Synonym: evolution

3. (biology) The process of an individual organism growing organically; a purely biological unfolding of events involved in an organism changing gradually from a simple to a more complex level
   "He discussed bone development in children."
   —Synonyms: growth, growing, maturation, ontogeny, ontogenesis

4. A recent event that has some relevance for the present situation
   "recent developments in Iraq"; "What a revolting development!"

5. The act of making some area of land or water more profitable or productive or useful
   "the development of Alaskan resources"
   —Synonym: exploitation

6. A district that has been developed to serve some purpose
   "Such land is practical for small park developments."

7. A state in which things are improving; the result of developing (as in the early part of a game of chess)
   "After he saw the latest development he changed his mind and became a supporter.";
   "In chess you should take care of your development before moving your queen."

8. Processing a photosensitive material in order to make an image visible
   "The development and printing of his pictures took only two hours."
   —Synonym: developing

9. (music) The section of a composition or movement (especially in sonata form) where the major musical themes are developed and elaborated

---

root

Noun
1. (botany) The usually underground organ that lacks buds or leaves or nodes; absorbs water and mineral salts; usually anchors the plant to the ground

2. The place where something begins, where it springs into being
   "communism's Russian root"
   —Synonyms: beginning, origin, rootage, source

3. (linguistics) The form of a word after all affixes are removed
   "Thematic vowels are part of the root."
   —Synonyms: root word, base, stem, theme, radical

4. A number that, when multiplied by itself some number of times,
   equals a given number

5. The set of values that gives a true statement when substituted into an equation
   —Synonym: solution

6. Someone from whom you are descended (but usually more remote than a
   grandparent)
   —Synonyms: ancestor, ascendant, ascendent, antecedent

7. A simple form inferred as the common basis from which related words in several
   languages can be derived by linguistic processes
   —Synonym: etymology

8. The part of a tooth that is embedded in the jaw and serves as support
   —Synonym: tooth root

Verb
9. Take root and begin to grow
   "This plant roots quickly."

10. Come into existence, originate
    "The problem roots in her depression."

11. Plant by the roots

12. Dig with the snout
    "The pig was rooting for truffles."
    —Synonym: rout

13. Become settled or established and stable in one's residence or life style
    "He finally rooted down."

14. Settle, take root, steady down, settle down

15. To give encouragement to a team or contestant; to lend support
    to a person or cause
    "They began to root for their team."

NOTES:

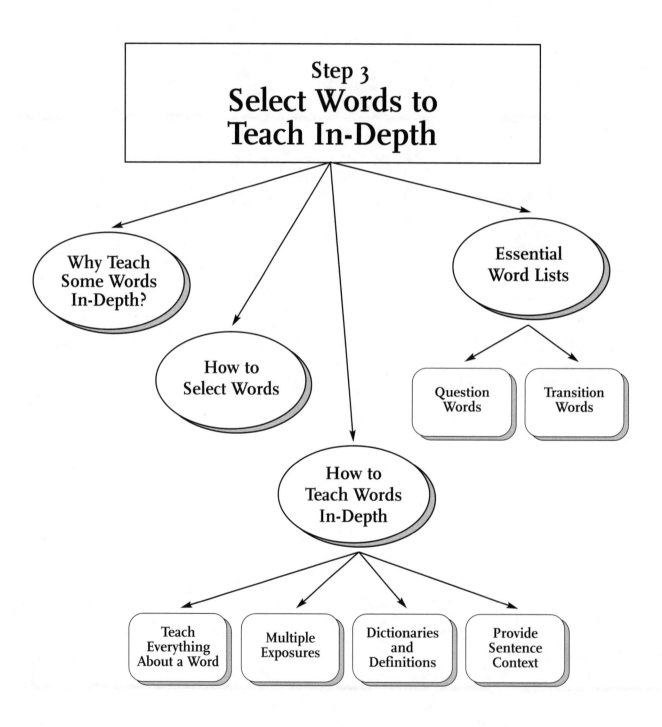

Step 3
**Select Words to
Teach In-Depth**

Why Teach
Some Words
In-Depth?

How to
Select Words

Essential
Word Lists

Question
Words

Transition
Words

How to
Teach Words
In-Depth

Teach
Everything
About a Word

Multiple
Exposures

Dictionaries
and
Definitions

Provide
Sentence
Context

Step 3: Select Specific Words to Teach In-Depth

Why Teach Some Words In-Depth?

In Chapter 2, it was noted that students must learn between 2000 and 3500 words per year. Wide reading is a major way for students to acquire these words, but a combination of direct and indirect methods of instruction is also necessary to build vocabulary. Direct methods of vocabulary instruction include teaching students strategies for learning new words such as analyzing word parts and using the context and promoting word consciousness. Direct vocabulary instruction also means selecting specific words to teach in-depth.

Providing direct instruction in key content vocabulary words is essential for students with weak vocabularies who struggle with reading. They are less likely to read extensively which is the only way they will have enough multiple exposures to essential academic words that are not commonly spoken. Graves (2006) provides several reasons why we should directly teach words:

> Teaching individual words pays a number of important dividends. First, and most obviously, teaching a child a word leaves him with one less word to learn independently. Second, teaching individual words gives students a store of words that they can use to explore and understand their environment. Third, teaching individual words can increase students' comprehension of selections containing those words. Fourth, and very importantly, teaching individual words demonstrates our interest in words, and teaching them in engaging and interesting ways fosters students' interest in words (p. 59).

Content area classrooms provide the best opportunities to teach words in-depth. A report from the Institute of Education Sciences (Kamil, et al., 2008) notes the following about content vocabulary instruction:

> Teachers should provide students with explicit vocabulary instruction both as part of reading and language arts classes and as part of content area classes such as science and social studies. ... In many content area texts it is the vocabulary that carries a large share of the meaning through specialized vocabulary, jargon, and discipline related concepts. Learning these specialized vocabularies contributes to the success of reading among adolescent students. Research has shown that integrating explicit vocabulary instruction into the existing curriculum of subject areas such as science or social studies enhances students' ability to acquire textbook vocabulary (p. 11).

Given the enormous number of vocabulary words that must be learned each year, it would not be possible to thoroughly teach all of them. The challenge lies in identifying which words to choose for cursory review and which to choose for in-depth instruction. In-depth teaching of every word that a teacher wants to preview or introduce is not necessary or practical. Providing a simple definition can be sufficient for words that are easy to explain or that do not need to be well known. However, it is useful to identify a set of key vocabulary words to teach in-depth, and research has found that direct instruction of at least 400 words per year (i.e., 10 words per week during the school year) produces gains in vocabulary and comprehension (Beck et al., 2002; Biemiller, 2004).

How to Select Words to Teach In-Depth

What words should the teacher choose for direct instruction? With so many words that students may not know, teachers can understandably be confused about which words to select. In general, teachers should focus on words that students will actually read, that are important to the text, useful to know in many situations, and that are uncommon in everyday spoken language but recurrent in books (Juel & Deffes, 2004).

As noted in Chapter 2, teachers should not rely on basal reading series or textbooks to identify words that should be taught. The choice of words for in-depth instruction must be made by the teacher, keeping in mind the particular needs of the students (e.g., grade level, literacy skills, English as a second language), the purpose of the reading, and the content instructional goals (e.g., is this a topic that is essential to the content curriculum?). In fact, words selected from the same reading may be different for students in one school than from another school, or even from one class to another within the same school. There is no right or wrong list of words to select; teachers must use their own best judgment.

Researchers have proposed several criteria for determining a smaller set of words to teach in-depth, but they all tend to focus on the following factors (Lehr et al., 2004):

- Words that are essential to understand the major concepts of the content topic and reading selection

- Words that are practical to know

- Words that students are likely to encounter again as they read and learn more about the content topic

There are several points to consider when choosing words to teach. Begin by reading the material and identifying the goals of the reading and classroom lesson to which the reading is connected. Keep these goals in mind:

- Select only words that are essential to the instructional goal. Unfamiliar words that are essential to comprehending the text but not essential to the instructional goal can be previewed but do not need to be selected for in-depth instruction.

- Select major concept words that are key to making connections between main ideas and building a schema for the subject of your instructional focus.

- Select words that will be frequently encountered in other reading material and that may help in other content areas.

- Select words that are unlikely to be learned independently through the use of the context or word analysis.

- Select words that provide good opportunities to practice word-learning strategies, such as using the context and analyzing word parts

- Select words that are unique and will increase student curiosity and interest in learning new words.

Beck, McKeown, and Kucan (2002) developed a useful model for categorizing words readers encounter in texts and for learning content. It is called the Three Tier model. The tiers are based on a word's commonality (more to less frequently occurring) and applicability (broader to narrower). The Common Core State Standards (2010) refer to this model in the review of the research supporting key elements of the standards:

> *While the term* tier *may connote a hierarchy, a ranking of words from least to most important, the reality is that all three tiers of words are vital to comprehension and vocabulary development, although learning tier two and three words typically requires more deliberate effort than does learning tier one words.*

Figure A presents the Three Tier model. Beck and McKeown note that the notion of tiers of words is not a precise one. In fact, some words may be considered Tier 1 words for some students and Tier 2 for other students. Some words within Tier 2 will be more familiar and useful than others.

Figure A

Beck and McKeown (2002) Three Tier Model

Tier 1	The words of everyday speech usually learned in the early grades. They are not considered a challenge to most students, though English language learners may have some difficulty with them. Tier 1 words should generally not be chosen to teach in-depth.
Tier 2	General academic words, high-frequency words that appear often in texts and are found across a variety of domains. Teachers need to determine which Tier 2 words need to be taught in-depth.
Tier 3	Uncommon, low-frequency words, usually specific to a domain or field of study. Tier 3 words are far more common in informational texts than in literature. Teachers need to determine which Tier 3 words need to be taught in-depth because they are essential to understanding and learning content.

provide with multiple exposure

Adapted from Beck, I.L, McKeown, M.G., and Kucan, L. (2002). *Bringing words to life: Robust vocabulary instruction.* New York: The Guilford Press.

Because Tier 3 words are obviously unfamiliar to most students, contain the ideas necessary to a new topic, and are recognized as both important and specific to the subject area, teachers should define these words prior to when students encounter them in a text and then reinforce their acquisition throughout a lesson (Common Core State Standards, 2010). The process of word acquisition occurs up to four times faster for Tier 3 words when students have become familiar with the content subject and encounter the word in different contexts (Landauer & Dumais, 1997; Common Core Standards, 2010). This is why *The Key Vocabulary Routine* emphasizes choosing and teaching words to teach in-depth based on what is being read and learned in the content classroom. The activities in Step 2 of the routine help students connect new words to existing subject area schema (background knowledge).

Tier 2 words, which by definition are not unique to a particular content area, tend to be far less well-defined by context clues when they appear in text and are far less likely to be defined explicitly within a text than are Tier 3 words. Because they are not unique to a particular content area, the responsibility for teaching these words may be less obvious to a content area teacher (Common Core State Standards, 2010). Although it may be easier to identify Tier 3 words to teach in-depth, content teachers must also consider Tier 2 words.

Teachers can also let students play a role in selecting which words to learn in-depth. Haggard (1982, as noted in Billmeyer & Barton, 1998) suggests the following activity for letting students select their own words by previewing the readings:

> Working in teams, students develop a list of unfamiliar terms that they believe will be crucial for understanding the focus of the unit. Student selected words are listed on chart paper, and each team is asked to defend its selections. The teacher then modifies this list by deleting terms judged to be less important and adding any vocabulary concepts that students overlooked. She clearly explains her reasons for including certain words and eliminating others so that students understand how to identify crucial words in content reading. (p. 22)

Stahl proposed three levels of increasingly complex word knowledge (Stahl, 1986; Marzano, 2004):

- **Association:** Students can make accurate associations about a word even if they do not understand the meaning of a word.

- **Comprehension:** Students understand the commonly accepted meaning of a word.

- **Generation:** Students can provide the word in a novel context.

These levels correspond nicely with the headings in the Word Knowledge Checklist provided in Step 1 of *The Key Vocabulary Routine*. Teachers can use the checklist or the three descriptive terms above to help students identify and discuss words they believe should be selected for in-depth study.

Activity 1: Practice Selecting Words

Directions: Use the list of words you generated for previewing. Using the Three Tier model and the suggestions provided above, select a subset of between 5-8 words to teach in-depth. Then answer the questions.

Selected Words:

1. _____   5. _____

2. _____   6. _____

3. _____   7. _____

4. _____   8. _____

1. Which students did you have in mind as you were selecting the words (i.e., grade level, skill level, etc.)?

_____

_____

_____

_____

2. Explain why you chose some words and left out others.

_____

_____

_____

_____

How to Teach Words In-Depth

Teachers need to provide what is called "rich vocabulary instruction" (Beck et al., 1987; 2002), which emphasizes long-term instruction of vocabulary that includes many encounters with a word and significant discussion and use of a word. Content classrooms offer an opportunity for students to have purposeful interaction with new vocabulary words in a content-rich environment. The National Reading Panel (2000) concluded:

Repeated exposure to vocabulary items is important for learning gains. The best gains were made in instruction that extended beyond single class periods and involved multiple exposures in authentic contexts beyond the classroom....Vocabulary learning is effective when it entails active engagement in the learning tasks (p. 4-4).

Teachers should help students learn how to use selected words in meaningful ways and in different contexts. In order to provide rich instruction, McKeown and Beck (2007, pp 185-187) suggest the following:

1. Introduce words through explanations in everyday connected language, rather than dictionary definitions.

2. Provide several contexts in which the word can be used.

3. Get students to interact with word meanings right away.

4. Develop activities that require students to process the meanings of words in deep and thoughtful ways (e.g., semantic mapping, categorizing, semantic feature analysis, scaling).

5. Provide examples, situations, and questions that are interesting.

6. Provide many encounters with target words.

Studies have shown that students learn vocabulary through discussion about text in the content classroom. A recent report from the Institute of Education Sciences (Kamil et al., 2008) summed up the positive effects of discussion of text vocabulary:

One study showed that discussion improved knowledge of word meanings and relationships for students reading biology texts.... Discussion seems to have its effects by allowing students to participate as both speakers and listeners.... It also presents opportunities for repeated exposure to words, shown to be a necessary condition for vocabulary learning (p.13).

Teach Everything About A Word

Knowledge of a word means knowing much more than its definition(s). Words can have multiple meanings depending on the context, function as different parts of speech, and share a root word with other words that have different suffixes and prefixes. In fact, seventy percent of the most frequently used words have multiple meanings (Bromley, 2007).

It is also important to learn the correct spelling and pronunciation of a word, especially if it is a word that sounds similar to another word. For example, *anecdote* and *antidote* differ only by two sounds (phonemes) in the middle of the word. *Specific* as compared to *pacific* has one extra sound (phoneme) at the beginning of the word.

Louisa Moats (2005) notes that words have phonological form (sounds, syllables), morphological form (meaningful parts), spelling patterns (orthographic form), meanings and meaning networks, syntactic roles, and linguistic history (etymological features). Students will acquire deeper knowledge about a word if they learn everything about it.

It is also useful to expose students to a nonlinguistic form of a new word, such as a picture of it or association of an object to the word, if possible. Paivio (1990) noted that information about words is "dual-coded" as it is stored in memory. That is, it is processed in linguistic form that includes print and meaning and nonlinguistic form that includes visual and sensory images (Bromley, 2007).

Here are three templates that can be used to help students learn a word in-depth. They all go beyond simply providing a dictionary definition for a word. The first is the *Frayer Method* (Frayer et al., 1969), a model that encourages students to analyze and discuss a key word's essential attributes and choose examples and non-examples of the concept. Figure B is an example of a Frayer Method template used for the word *nautical*.

Figure B

Frayer Method	Concept Word: *nautical*
Define the word, include picture if possible —*Related to shipping or navigation.* 	List key characteristics and attributes —*Associated with the ocean* —*Describes ships, sailors* —*Things that help travel over water*
Example —*Rigging and sails* —*Seamen* —*Rudder*	Non-example —*Mountains* —*Train* —*Paved roads*

Adapted from: Frayer, D.A., Frederick, W.D., & Klausmeier, H.J. (1969). *A schema for testing the level of concept mastery* (Technical Report No. 16). Madison: University of Wisconsin, Wisconsin Center for Education Research.

[handwritten note: Can put word in middle]

The second template for teaching different aspects of a word is a *Concept Definition Map* (Schwartz, 1988). With this activity, students are encouraged to apply personal knowledge to learn more about a word. Figure C is an example of a Concept Definition Map.

Can be[g] [to do] 20
hard to do

Figure C

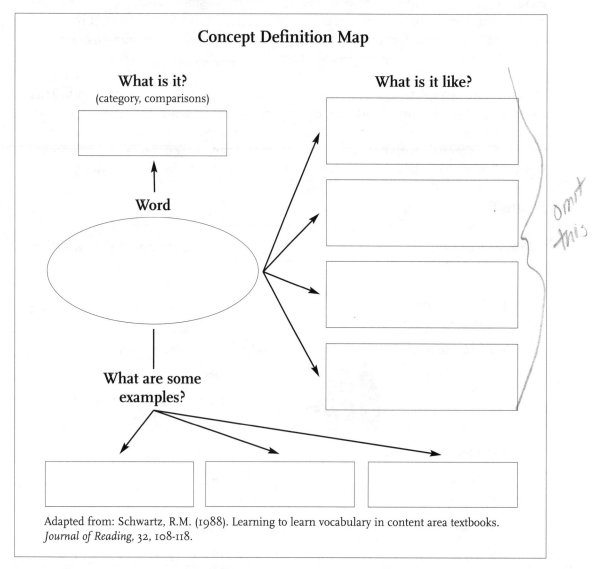

omit this

Adapted from: Schwartz, R.M. (1988). Learning to learn vocabulary in content area textbooks. *Journal of Reading*, 32, 108-118.

The third template for presenting different aspects of a word is the *Two-Column Notes Template* which is adapted from the two-column note taking format used in *The Key Comprehension Routine* (Sedita, 2010). With this template, a word is listed in the left column, and information about the word is listed in the right column (definitions, synonyms and antonyms, related words, examples/nonexamples, multiple meanings, sample sentence, illustration). There are several advantages to using this format. First, students can collect information about more than one word on a page. Second, the two-column format is efficient for reviewing vocabulary words. The information in the right column can be covered while the students read the word and quiz themselves on the information about the word. Similarly, students can cover the left side of the page, and try to remember the word based on information about the word in the right column. Figure D is an example of two-column notes for vocabulary. Note that not all of the items in the right column are applicable for every word (e.g., having an antonym or illustration). In those cases, students can enter NA for not *applicable*.

Figure D

Two-Column Notes Template

word	Definition: Part of speech: Synonym: Antonym: Category/related words: Example: Nonexample: Multiple meanings: Sentence: Illustration:

Here is an example of how the two-column template can be used for the vocabulary words *lexicon, migrate,* and *nautical*.

lexicon	**Definition:** *a language user's knowledge of words* **Part of speech:** *noun* **Synonym:** *dictionary, glossary* **Antonym:** *NA* **Category/related words:** *vocabulary, words, definition, meaning* **Example:** *The words I use to speak.* **Nonexample:** *NA* **Multiple meanings:** *inventory or record* **Sentence:** *Because the boy read every night, he developed a large lexicon and knew more words than most of his friends.* **Illustration:**

migrate	**Definition:** *to move from one country or area and settle in another*
	Part of speech: *verb*
	Synonym: *move*
	Antonym: *stay*
	Category/related words: *travel, movement, different places, relocate, immigrants, settlers, pilgrimage*
	Example: *The Pilgrims migrated to the New World.*
	Nonexample: *The man stayed in the same house his whole life.*
	Multiple meanings: *migration – passage of a group of animals such as birds from one region to another for breeding or feeding*
	Sentence: *The migration of many settlers from the East by covered wagon helped populate the West.*
	Illustration: 
nautical	**Definition:** *related to shipping or navigation of a body of water*
	Part of speech: *adjective*
	Synonym: *maritime, naval*
	Antonym: *land*
	Category/related words: *marine, ocean, boat, sailor*
	Example: *Sails on a boat.*
	Nonexample: *car, train*
	Multiple meanings: *NA*
	Sentence: *The museum had a collection of nautical items that included ship parts and items used by sailors to navigate while crossing the ocean.*
	Illustration:

If you make a template two — top & bottom front & back fit of words

Activity 2: Practice Teaching a Word In-Depth

Directions: Work with a partner. Choose one of the words you selected in Activity 1. Use the Frayer Method, a Concept Definition Map, or the Two-Column Notes Template to teach the word to your partner.

Provide Multiple Exposures to Words

As noted in Chapter 2, learning a word is a long-term process that involves many encounters with the word. In addition to needing repeated exposure to words, students also need practice using them in different contexts. Teachers should therefore strive to identify opportunities to revisit words that have been selected for instruction beyond just the first day that they are introduced. The more often a student encounters a word, and the closer together the encounters occur, the greater the chance that the word will be learned and remembered. Frequent exposures should be as meaningful as possible, including links to previous information about the word and student discussion about the word as it may relate to different situations. When lesson planning, teachers should try to find ways to use the new words repeatedly, to point out and model the use of the words, and to do so over multiple days of instruction.

Using Dictionaries and Definitions

We now know from Chapter 2 that having students look up and memorize definitions is one of the least effective strategies for acquiring new words. Also, because conventional dictionary definitions can be hard to understand, students often cannot use them to learn words. This does not mean that students should not use dictionaries. However, their use should be limited and students must be taught how to use a dictionary effectively.

Effective use of a dictionary should include teacher modeling and thinking aloud about how to look up a word and select an appropriate definition for a particular context (Lehr, et al, 2004). Teachers need to provide explicit instruction about how to read and use the parts of dictionary entries (e.g., multiple meanings, parts of speech, pronunciation, etymology).

Teachers should be sure they are providing grade-level appropriate dictionaries. They should also consider introducing students to alternative dictionaries that contain more user-friendly definitions. The Collins Co-Build dictionaries (http://www.collinslanguage.com) are examples of dictionaries with word entries that are easy to understand and examples of the word in sentences that provide context. Here are some examples from the Co-Build dictionary:

- *carat:* A *carat* is a unit equal to 0.2 grams used for measuring the weight of diamonds and other precious stones.

- *exclude:* If you *exclude* someone from a place or activity, you prevent them from entering it or taking part in it.

Using a thesaurus to find synonyms for a new word can sometimes be a better alternative to standard dictionary entries. Another online resource is Word Web (http://www.wordwebonline.com/) which offers free online dictionary and thesaurus features that provide user-friendly definitions as well as synonyms and antonyms for words.

The best approach to definitions is to have students generate their own using easy to understand, everyday language. A student definition should include the word, a linking verb, a superordinate or category for the word, and relative clauses that contain important attributes of the word. Moats (2005) suggests this formula for developing a student definition:

A _____ is (a) _____ that (is, does) _____ .
      (word)   (category, synonym)   (attributes)

This formula can be adapted for use with various parts of speech (not just nouns), as follows:

A *noun* is a ____ that ____.

To *verb* is to _____ by/such as ____.

To be *adjective* is to ____.

To do something *adverb* is to _____.

Here are some examples of student definitions for words that are various parts of speech:

Nouns

An *eagle* is a large bird that soars in the sky, catches small prey, and has been named as the symbol of the United States.

A *decoy* is a live or artificial animal used to entice another animal into a trap or within shooting range.

Verbs

To **yell** is to make a loud sound by using one's voice such as a scream.

To **defeat** is to win a victory over something, such as beating another sports team or winning a battle.

Adjectives

To be **wealthy** is to have a lot of material possessions such as money or valuables.

Something **magical** is mysterious and related to supernatural forces, charms, or spells.

Adverbs

To do something **curtly** is to do it in a rude and abrupt way.

To do something **quickly** is to do it fast and react immediately.

Provide Sentence Context for New Words

Students will learn a word more readily if they can see how that word is used in context. Sometimes the reading from which the word was selected provides a good context clue. If this is the case, students should copy the sentence or passage into their vocabulary notes. If not, the students can generate sample sentences that demonstrate an understanding of what the word means.

Asking students to use a new vocabulary word in a sentence has been standard practice in many classrooms for years. However, we all know students will often generate sentences that do not express the meaning of a word. Also, when students put words into sentences, they often use them as the wrong part of speech, or miss the subtle nuances of meaning. One way to avoid this is to require students to use the student definition formulas noted above. Another way is to ask students to combine two or more new vocabulary words into a sentence or paragraph. To complete this task, students have to think about the meanings of the words and how they can relate them to generate a sentence that makes sense. This is called sentence synthesis and, in addition to supporting vocabulary development, it also builds logical thinking. Here is an example using the two words, *migrate* and *nautical:*

In order to *migrate* from England to the New World, early colonists needed *nautical* knowledge to be able to sail across the Atlantic Ocean.

To scaffold this exercise, teachers can generate sentences with blanks for a list of words.

The students must determine which word best fits in the sentence given their knowledge of the word. Here is an example using *lexicon, migrate,* and *nautical:*

To _____ is when people move from one place or one country to another.

A _____ is a collection of words such as a dictionary or set of words that an author uses when writing.

Something is _____ if it is related to sailing or navigating a body of water such as the ocean.

Essential Word Lists for Content Learning

Question words and transition words are essential for any subject area. Teachers should provide opportunities to expose students to these words on a regular basis.

Question Words
Teaching students to answer and generate questions has been identified as a highly effective strategy for improving comprehension (National Reading Panel, 2000). We also know that in order to perform well on many high stakes tests students must be familiar with question words that are used in open response and other types of test questions. Sometimes even the most common question words must be taught directly to students. Figure E is a list of question words that is adapted from *The Key Comprehension Routine* (Sedita, 2010). In this program students are taught how to generate questions at the different levels of Bloom's taxonomy.

Transition Words
Transition words are useful for connecting sentences or paragraphs, and students should be familiar with them to support reading comprehension and writing. Figure F is a list of common transition words that are used in *The Key Comprehension Routine* for use when writing summaries.

For both the question and transition word lists, teachers should find opportunities to provide direct and explicit instruction through modeling and guided practice for how these words are used. Posters or word wall lists of these words is one way to create awareness and encourage students to use them.

Figure E

Question Words

adapt	describe	infer	relate
agree	design	integrate	repeat
analyze	develop	invent	rephrase
apply	differentiate	interpret	represent
appraise	disagree	judge	rewrite
arrange	discriminate	label	select
assess	discuss	list	show
associate	dispute	match	simplify
calculate	dissect	measure	solve
categorize	distinguish	model	substitute
choose	divide	modify	summarize
clarify	elaborate	name	support
classify	estimate	omit	tabulate
compare	evaluate	order	tell
complete	examine	organize	test
compile	explain	outline	theorize
compose	experiment	paraphrase	use
conclude	extend	plan	utilize
connect	find	predict	what
contrast	formulate	prepare	what if
construct	generalize	produce	when
convince	generate	propose	where
create	give examples	quote	which
criticize	identify	rank	who
decide	illustrate	rearrange	why
defend	imagine	recall	
define	implement	recognize	
demonstrate	improve	recommend	

Adapted from: Sedita, J. (2003). *The Key Three Routine: Comprehension Strategy Instruction*. Danvers, MA: Keys to Literacy.

Figure F

Transition Words and Phrases

To indicate a time relationship	after, afterward, after that, at first, at this time, before, beginning with, beyond, during, earlier, ending with, eventually, finally, following, from then on, in the meantime, last, later, meanwhile, next, now, since, soon, then, until, while
To indicate spatial placement	below, beside, between, beyond, farther on, here, next to, parallel with
To list or present a series of ideas	after, after that, finally, first, lastly, next, second, third
To add information or continue a line of thought	also, another, besides, further, furthermore, in addition, likewise, moreover, similarly
To summarize or show conclusion	accordingly, finally, in conclusion, in other words, in short, to conclude, to sum up, to summarize
To show comparison	by comparison, compared to, in like manner, likewise, similarly
To show contrast	although, but, however, in contrast, nevertheless, on the contrary, on the other hand, unlike
To repeat information or stress a point	above all, in fact, in other words, most important, once again, to repeat
To provide an example or illustrate a point	for example, for instance, such as, to illustrate, that is
To show cause and effect	as a result, because, because of, caused by, consequently, for that reason, that is why, therefore, thus
To state the obvious	certainly, granted that, in fact, most certainly, naturally, obviously, of course, surely, undoubtedly, without a doubt

Step 3 Summary

In addition to building vocabulary through indirect methods such as wide reading, teachers should also select and identify specific words to teach directly. Because there are so many words that students may not know, it is important to apply criteria for selecting a smaller set of words to teach in-depth. Once those words have been identified, students must learn everything about them including their sounds, spelling, and multiple meanings. Multiple exposure to these words over time, together with student-friendly definitions, are necessary for students to truly learn them.

NOTES:

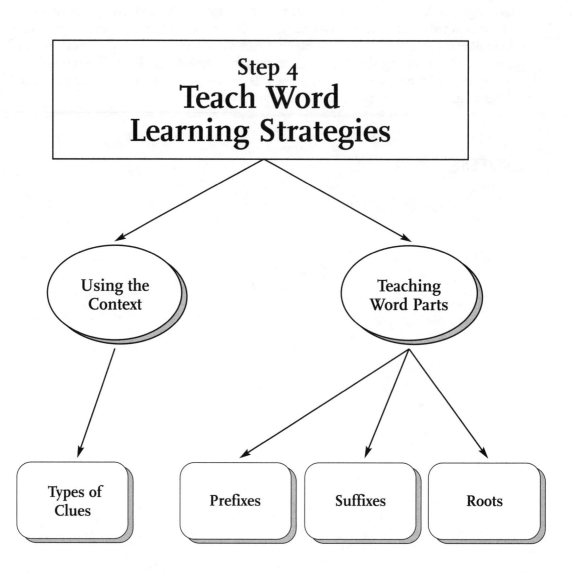

Step 4: Identify Opportunities to Teach Word Learning Strategies

One component of effective vocabulary instruction is to directly teach students how to use context and word analysis skills to infer the meanings of new words. Carlisle (2007) maintains that incidental word learning through contextual clues and morphological analysis (knowledge of word parts) is the primary means through which students acquire new vocabulary. Frey and Fisher (2011) suggest teaching students to "Look inside the word and outside the word to see what you know". When used in tandem, use of word parts (inside the word) and use of context (outside the word) can be very helpful. Figure A represents the combined strategies.

Figure A

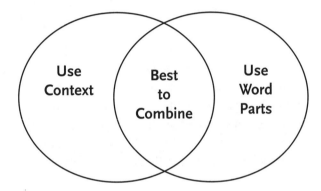

Baumann and his colleagues (2003, 2005) developed and studied the effectiveness of an instructional strategy called the Vocabulary Rule that combines the use of context clues and word part clues. They concluded that students can be taught both approaches and that combined instruction is as effective as separate instruction. Diamond and Gutlohn (2006) developed the chart in Figure B based upon Baumann's combined approach. The steps in the process include using context and word parts to derive the meaning of a word, and then using a dictionary to confirm the meaning.

Figure B

The Vocabulary Strategy

> To figure out the meaning of an unfamiliar word that you come across while reading:
> _____
>
> 1. **Look for context clues** in the words, phrases, and sentences surrounding the unfamiliar word
>   - A. Try to break the word into parts. (If you can't, skip to Step 3.)
>   - B. Look at the root word. What does it mean?
>   - C. Look at the prefix. What does it mean?
>   - D. Look at the suffix. What does it mean?
>   - E. Put the meanings of the word parts together. What is the meaning of the whole word?

---

3. Guess the word's meaning (Use Steps 1 and 2.)

---

4. Try out your meaning in the original sentence to check whether or not it makes sense in context

---

5. Use the dictionary, if necessary, to confirm your meaning

Diamond, L. & Gutlohn, L. (2006). *Vocabulary handbook*. Baltimore, MD: Paul H. Brookes.

This chapter will address use of context and use of word parts individually – but in practice, students should be encouraged to use the two strategies simultaneously.

Using the Context

Good readers can use context clues, if they are available, to determine the meaning of unfamiliar words. They can locate other words or phrases in the passage that give clues to the meaning of an unknown word. Expository, non-fiction text tends to offer more context clues than narrative text. A number of studies have shown that when students are taught to use context clues they become better at figuring out the definitions of words compared to students who are not directly taught this skill (Kuhn & Stahl, 1998).

The best way to teach students how to use the context is to provide many examples from content reading. One suggestion to help students become more aware of using context is to identify text they are reading as being "rich in context" (i.e., has a lot of clues to figure out a word) or "lean in context" (i.e., not much there to figure out a word).

There are different types of context clues, including the following types of information that may be embedded in the text: definition, description, synonym, comparison, contrast, or example. Figure C provides examples of these different types of context clues.

As noted above, teachers need to provide direct and explicit instruction for how the context can be used to infer the meaning of new words. It was noted in Step 3 of *The Key Vocabulary Routine* that seventy percent of the most frequently used words have multiple meanings (Bromley, 2007). The context often helps students determine the specific meaning for the word in a particular text. Graves (2006, p. 99) suggests teaching students the following four-step strategy for inferring words from context:

1. Read carefully and ask yourself, "Does this make sense?"

2. Notice when you don't know the meaning of a word and slow down. Read that sentence at least once more, looking for clues.

3. If necessary, go back and reread the preceding sentence, looking for clues that help you figure out what the word might mean.

Figure C

Types of Contextual Clues		
Type of Clue	**Explanation**	**Example**
Definition	The word is defined directly in the sentence.	The nation was undergoing **urbanization** – the movement of people into cities. One result of this motion is **diffusion**, the net movement of the particles of a substance from where they are more concentrated to where they are less concentrated.
Description	The word is described by information in the context so that the reader can figure out the meaning.	**Pollination** occurs when a pollen grain from a male plant lands on the stigma of a female plant. Cities were filling with immigrants and newcomers from American farms and small towns. Too poor to rent their own apartments, they shared rooms and crammed together in **tenements.**
Synonym	A word that is similar to the word is provided.	Water soaks into the ground **pores**, or **spaces**, among the fragments of soil. It was a **triptych**, or **three-paneled**, painting.
Comparison	The word is compared with other examples that are similar.	Light enters your eye through a **pupil**, which is like a small hole. **Cumulus** clouds look like a pile of cotton balls.
Contrast	The word is contrasted with another word, usually an antonym.	Unlike a **compound**, an **element** cannot be broken down into simpler materials. Volunteering to join the army offers the choice that a **draftee** does not have.
Example	A word or words that are examples are provided.	An example of **mutualism** is the pea crab and the mussel. Tiny pea crabs live inside mussel shells. The crabs eat the young of organisms that would harm the mussels if they grew to adults inside the shell. In return, the mussels provide protection for the little crabs. The children could tell, from Phil's statement about everything and everybody having a good side, that he was an **optimist.**

Most Confusing*

*

4. When you figure out what the word might mean, substitute your guess for the difficult word and see if it makes sense. If it does, keep on reading. If it doesn't, try again.

It is important to point out that not all contexts are helpful. Contexts vary in how much information they provide a reader. Sometimes the context provides a direct explanation of the meaning of a new word. Here are two examples from middle school textbooks:

Example: Up to this point we have been referring to the process in which light energy is used to make food simply as the food-making process. But this important process has its own special name: *photosynthesis*.

In this example, the meaning of *photosynthesis* is directly stated in the previous sentence.

Example: Prince Henry started a school for sea captains. These captains were taught the science of *navigation*. That is, they were taught how to figure out a ship's location and the direction and distance that it travels.

In this example, the meaning of *navigation* is stated directly in the next sentence.

Sometimes the context provides some information about a new word but not enough for the student to be aware of its full meaning. Here are two more examples from middle school textbooks:

Example: In order to gain active immunity to a disease, one of two things must occur – either you come down with the disease, or you receive a *vaccination*.

In this example, the student may guess that a *vaccination* has something to do with preventing disease, but there is not enough information to discern just what a vaccination is.

Example: Cartier found the mouth of a large river, which he named the St. Lawrence River. He sailed up this river until he came to a *rapid*. Ships cannot pass across a *rapid*. Disappointed, Cartier had to turn back.

In this example, the student may guess that a *rapid* is something in a river that prohibits a ship from passing, but not enough information is provided to identify specifically what is impeding the ship's progress.

While the context may sometimes be helpful, research shows that when readers attempt to derive the meanings of words in context they may get them wrong (Pressley et al., 2007). This may be because the student does not have enough prior knowledge to make sense of the clues in the text, or it may be that the clues are misleading. Beck, McKeown, and Kucan (2002) have identified some text as "misdirective" (i.e., leading to a misunderstanding). They caution that while students should be taught how to use context clues, they should not be given the impression that meaning can be readily derived from all contexts. Here is an example of a misdirective from their book *Bringing Words to Life:*

> **Example:** "Sandra had won the dance contest, and the audience's cheers brought her to the stage for an encore. 'Every step she takes is so perfect and graceful,' Ginny said *grudgingly* as she watched Sandra dance." (p. 4)

> In this example, the student might wrongfully assume that Ginny admired Sandra's dancing.

The instructional conclusion about teaching students how to use the context is that direct and explicit instruction should be given, and examples of clues in context should be pointed out to students during content classroom reading. However, teachers must be careful not to rely on using the context as their primary way of teaching vocabulary. They should make students aware that this approach has its limitations.

Activity 1: Practice Using the Context

Part 1

Directions: Using a sample of your content classroom reading material, skim to find examples where the context can be used to help determine the meaning of the word. Try to identify which type of context clue was provided.

Words	Page Number	Type of Clue
_____	_____	_____
_____	_____	_____
_____	_____	_____
_____	_____	_____
_____	_____	_____

Part 2

Directions: Develop a mini-lesson plan that uses these examples to model and explicitly teach context clues.

_____

_____

_____

_____

_____

_____

_____

Teaching Word Parts

When students encounter unknown words they can sometimes use knowledge of word parts (i.e., roots, suffixes, and prefixes) to help determine the meaning of the word. Content textbooks in particular contain related words that are derived from the same Latin or Greek root. For example, the root *bio* (meaning *life, living organisms*) reappears again and again in science text (e.g., *biology, biologist, biosphere, biodegradable, biochemical, biohazard,* etc.). Another example is the prefix *mono* (meaning *one, alone, single*). If students are familiar with the meaning of this prefix, and the base word *theism* (meaning *belief in the existence of a god or gods*), they may infer that *monotheism* means the belief in one god. Structural analysis of a word draws the student's attention to the individual units of meaning in a word, also known as morphemes.

Carlisle (2007, p. 79) notes that a large percentage of the words students learn after the third grade are derived words, such as *discontinuous (dis + continue + ous)* that have a base word with one or more affixes (prefixes or suffixes) that change the meaning and grammatical role of the word. Nagy and Anderson (1984) estimated that 60% of the unfamiliar words middle school students encounter in books are derived words whose meaning could be figured out by analysis of word structure and their use in the passage.

Morphemes and Morphological Awareness

Morphemes are the smallest units of meaning in a language. Some morphemes are *free* – they can stand alone (e.g., cat, walk, govern). Other morphemes are *bound* – they cannot stand alone (e.g., re-, un-, geo, tele, -ed, -ment). Morphemes are combined in different ways to express particular meaning or to fill grammatical roles. For example, the word parts in the chart below can be combined to create the following words: *whenever, however, whatever, whoever, every, everything, everybody, everyone, everywhere.* Morphological awareness refers to recognizing the presence of morphemes in words.

when how what who	ever	y	thing body one where

Research suggests that students can be taught various morphemic elements as a way to determine the meaning of new words (Edwards et al., 2004). Carlisle (2010) analyzed 16 studies about the relation of morphological awareness instruction to key components of literacy development. The findings showed that instruction about word parts was associated with improvements in word reading or spelling, and in determining the meaning of unfamiliar words.

A compound word is a word that combines two morphemes to create a separate, new word. Here are some examples:

Basic compounds: *songbird, sandbox, flashlight*
Compound phrases: *polar ice cap*
Hyphenated: *red-headed woodpecker, son-in-law, self-esteem*
Open compounds: *ice cube, book jacket, swing set*
Compound roots: *manuscript, telescope*

In the upper elementary grades, there are many opportunities to find words in content reading that contain Greek and Latin morphemes. However, children in primary grades can begin to learn how morphemes combine by adding prefixes and suffixes to short Anglo-Saxon words and also compounding them. For example:

jump, jumps, jumped, jumping, jumper
read, reread, reader, nonreader, reading
sunshine, schoolhouse, upstream

There are some limitations to morphemic analysis. Although it is useful, teachers must also make students aware that it doesn't *always* work. This is because some prefixes are not consistent in meaning (e.g., *in-* means both *not* and *in*). It is also because the meanings of many Greek and Latin roots have changed substantially over hundreds of years, so they no longer lend themselves to literal translation. For example, the literal translation of *circumspect* should be *look around* (*circum* means *around*, and *spect* means *look*), while the real meaning is *cautious, careful*.

Teaching Word Parts

One way to introduce word analysis skills is to teach students how words are made up of word parts, and how words can be related in word families. Edwards et al. (2004, p. 164-166) suggests four guidelines for teaching word analysis:

1. **Provide explicit instruction in how word analysis works.** Teach how parts function together to construct word meanings, and help students learn to locate meaningful parts of unfamiliar words.

2. **Use word families to promote vocabulary growth.** Teach a root word and its derived forms so students can see how knowing a word with the same root can help them make meaning for another word in the same family. Covering a family of words helps students see the types of changes that can occur among related words. (Figure D provides an example of a word family.)

3. **Promote independent use of word analysis.** The number of roots, suffixes, and prefixes is enormous, more than a teacher can cover in the classroom. Teachers should encourage independent learning of affix or root meanings.

4. **Enhance students' awareness that word analysis does not always work.** Word analysis can be a useful strategy, but it does not always work. Sometimes students can be misled by what may appear to be a word clue. For example, *unassuming* does not mean *not assuming*, and *discharge* does not mean the opposite of *charge*.

Often, opportune moments come up during content instruction to provide examples of word analysis skills. Words from a preview list may include common word parts, or an opportunity to make a connection between the root of a new word and a word previously covered in class may arise. Content teachers in particular are in a position to point out examples of words that contain roots, prefixes, and suffixes from content classroom reading material.

Figure D

Word Family for the Latin root *port* (to carry)

portability	deporting	imported	supporter
portable	deportment	importer	supporting
portableness		importing	supportive
portably	export		
portage	exportable	portfolio	transport
portapack	exportation		transportable
portative	exported	report	transportability
ported	exporter	reportable	transportation
porter	exporting	reportage	transporter
porterage		reported	transporting
porting		reportedly	transportive
	import	reporter	
	importable	reporting	
deport	importability		
deportable	importance		
deportation	important	support	
deported	importantly	supportable	
deportee	importation	supportably	

Activity 2: Practice with Word Parts

Directions
Step 1: *Review the list of preview words you generated in Step 1 of Routine and pull out any words that contain roots, prefixes, and suffixes.*

Words

_____   _____

_____   _____

_____   _____

Step 2: *Using a sample of your content classroom reading material (e.g., textbook, article, short story, etc.), skim one or two pages and identify words that contain roots, prefixes, and suffixes.*

Words

_____   _____

_____   _____

_____   _____

Step 3: *Select any of the words from above and create a family of associated words using different prefixes and suffixes.*

Word: _____

Words from the same family:

_____

_____

_____

There are three types of word parts that can be taught: prefixes (come before a root and change meaning), suffixes (come after the root and sometimes change the meaning), and base words or roots (the basic part of a word that carries the main meaning). Each of these is discussed below.

Teaching Prefixes

A prefix comes before a root or base word and changes its meaning. There is a significant body of research indicating that instruction of prefixes is beneficial, and many vocabulary researchers recommend instruction of the most common prefixes as the first and best component of word analysis (Graves, 2004; Edwards et al., 2004;

Carlisle, 2007). White, Sowell, and Yanagihara (1989) found that 20 prefixes account for almost 97% of the 2,959 prefixed words that most frequently appear in school reading materials, and four of them accounted for 58% of all prefixes (Edwards, et al., 2004). Given how often these 20 prefixes occur in words, it makes sense to teach their meaning and use. Figure E is a list of these prefixes.

Figure E

20 Most Common Prefixes Found in Frequently Used Prefixed Words

prefix	common meaning	examples	#words	percentage
un-	1. not 2. opposite of, contrary to	1. unhappy 2. unrest	782	26.4%
re-	1. again, anew 2. backwards, back	1. rebuild 2. react	401	13.6%
in-, im-, ir-, il-	1. not	1. inactive, immobile, irrational, illegal	313	10.6%
dis-	1. not 2. opposite of 3. remove	1. dissimilar 2. disfavor 3. discolor	216	7.3%
en-, em-	1. put or go into or onto 2. to cause to be	1. encage, embed 2. endear, emblaze	132	4.5%
non-	1. not	1. nonhuman	126	4.3%
in-, im-	1. into, inside, within	1.inbound, immerge, illuminate	105	3.5%
over-	1. above, too much	1. overuse	98	3.3%
mis-	1. bad, wrong 2. failure, lack	1. misconduct 2. misfire	83	2.8%
sub-	1. below, under 2. secondary 3. less than complete	1. subsoil 2. subplot 3. subhuman	80	2.7%
pre-	1. before, in front of	1. prehistoric	79	2.7%

inter-	1. between, among	1. international	77	2.6%
fore-	1. before, in front of	1. forerunner	76	2.5%
de-	1. make opposite of 2. remove 3. reduce	1. decriminalize 2. dethrone 3. declass	71	2.4%
trans-	1. across, beyond 2. change 3. through	1. transatlantic 2. transcribe 3. transfer	47	1.6%
super-	1. above, over 2. superior 3. excessive	1. superimpose 2. superfine 3. supercharge	43	1.5%
semi-	1. half 2. partial 3. happening two times during	1. semicircle 2. semiconscious 3. semimonthly	39	1.3%
anti-	1. opposite, counteracting	1. antigravity, antibody	33	1.1%
mid-	1. middle	1. midstream	33	1.1%
under-	1. beneath, below, less in degree	1. underage	25	.8%
		Total:	**2,859**	**96.6%**

Adapted from: White, T.G., Sowell, J., & Yanagihara, A. (1989). Teaching elementary students to use word-part clues. *The Reading Teacher, 42*, 302-308.

In addition to these common prefixes, there are some numeric prefixes that are helpful to know, especially for science and math content (Ebbers, 2006). Figure F is a list of numeric prefixes.

Figure F

Numerical Prefixes

Meaning	Greek	Latin	Examples
one	mono	uni	monotone, unicorn
two	di	bi, du, duo	dioxide, binoculars, duet
three	tri	tri	triangle, triplicate
four	tetra	quad (quart)	tetrahedron, quadruplets, quarter
five	penta	quint	pentagon, quintet
six	hexa	sext	hexagon, sextuplets
eight	octo	octo	octopus, octagon
ten	deca	deci	decathlon, decimal
hundred		cent	century
thousand	kilo	mille	kilometer, millenium
part, half	hemi	semi	hemisphere, semicolon
many	poly	multi	polygon, multifaceted

Adapted from: Ebbers, S. (2006). Linking the language. Self-published.

There are many instances where identifying a prefix and combining the knowledge of that prefix meaning with the meaning of the root will help students figure out the meaning of an unfamiliar word. However, as noted, this does not always work and sometimes students can be misled by what may appear to be a word clue. Here are a few tips for teaching prefixes:

1. Provide direct, explicit instruction about what a prefix is and how it can affect the meaning of a word. Provide many examples of words with prefixes that most students already know.

2. Avoid having students focus on memorizing the meanings of prefixes; instead, have them practice using knowledge of prefix meanings to help define new words.

3. Let students know that some prefixes can have more than one meaning. Also, the common meaning(s) of a prefix cannot always be translated literally. In many instances the common meaning provides just a clue to the full meaning of a word.

4. Encourage students to think of other words they know that start with the same prefix. This can provide another clue to the meaning.

5. Provide students lists of roots and prefixes and have them try to combine them to create words.

6. Let students know that the prefixes *in, im, ir* and *il* are just different spellings of the same prefix. Sometimes this occurs when the first letter of the root word begins with *n, m, r,* or *l* (e.g., *innumerable, immovable, irregular, illogical*).

7. Point out to students that not all words that start with the same letters as these prefixes actually contain the prefix (e.g., **un**cle, **rel**ative, **inf**ant, **disc**ipline)

8. As noted above, take advantage of opportune moments to point out prefixes when they appear in classroom reading material.

Teaching Suffixes

Suffixes come after a root word. There are two kinds of suffixes:

- **Inflectional suffixes:** change the form of a word but not its part of speech; includes verb forms *ed* and *ing* (e.g., hop, hopp*ed*, hopp*ing*), plurals (e.g., dog/dog*s*, ax/ax*es*), and comparatives and superlatives *er* and *est* (e.g., dark/dark*er*/dark*est*)

- **Derivational suffixes:** modify the meaning of a word and sometimes its part of speech (e.g., fear*less*, elec*tion*, bio*logy*)

Sometimes a root word may have several suffixes (e.g., *environmentalist:* environ + ment + al + ist).

While the usefulness of teaching prefixes is apparent, there is less agreement about the value of teaching suffixes (Stahl, 1999; Lehr et al., 2004). Inflectional suffixes (i.e., ed, ing, er, est, s, es) do not really change meaning and are so common that most students already know how to use them by the end of grade three. Word analysis skills for the sake of helping to make meaning should therefore focus on derivational suffixes.

Unfortunately, many suffixes have vague or unhelpful meanings, although there are some that have more stable meanings that are worth teaching. The natural conclusion is to identify and teach some suffixes that have obvious meanings and may be most useful in helping students determine the meaning of new words, but teachers should not spend a significant amount of time directly teaching suffixes. The emphasis should be on taking advantage of opportune situations when new words with suffixes present themselves in content classroom reading. Figure G is a suggested list of common, useful suffixes.

Figure G

Common, Useful Suffixes

Suffix	Meaning	Example
-able/-ible	capable of	believable, collectible
-al/-ial	pertaining to	personal
-ance	state or condition	performance
-ant	one who (occupation), a condition	consultant, compliant
-arium	a place for	aquarium
-ate	quality of, to act upon	literate, calculate
-cian	one who	musician
-ee/-eer	one who	employee, volunteer
-ent	causing an action, one who	absorbent, student
-er/-or	one who, that which	pitcher, inspector, clipper
-ful	full of	joyful
-ic	relating to or marked by	academic
-ion/-tion/-sion	a thing, noun; condition of	companion, intuition, passion, invasion, promotion
-ish	pertaining to, being	brownish
-ism	belief system, doctrine, practice	communism

-ist	believer in a system, doctrine	anarchist
-ity	state, quality of	abnormality
-ive/-tive/-ative	performing or tending toward a specific action	demonstrative
-ize	to cause to be or make	dramatize
-less	without	childless
-logy/-ology	study of	biology
-ly	resembling, having the quality of	happily
-ment	result of an action or process	excitement
-ness	quality or state of	softness
-ous, -ious, -cious	full of, having	joyous, curious, delicious

Teaching Base Words and Roots

A *base word* or *root* is the basic part of a word that carries the main component of meaning. The difference between a base word and a root is:

- A base word is usually a free-standing word, often of Anglo-Saxon origin (e.g., *water, drink, father*). It is often easier for students to figure out the meaning of base words with prefixes or suffixes (e.g., *underwater, drinkable, fatherless*).

- Roots are usually not free-standing, and often of Latin or Greek origin (e.g., *vis* as in *visual* or *envisage*, or *aqua* as in *aquamarine* or *semiaquatic*). Greek roots are often found in science and math text. Students are usually not ready to apply word analysis skills to these kinds of words until after grade three.

There are several reasons why it may not make sense to provide direct instruction of very many specific root words (Graves, 2006):

- There are thousands of root words, making it unrealistic to choose a reasonable number to teach directly.

- Roots, especially Latin, vary in how they are spelled in different words which makes it difficult to recognize them.

- The relationship between the original meaning of the word and the current meaning of the English word in which it is used is often vague.

- There may only be a few commonly used words that contain any given root word.

On the other hand, a significant number of words that students will encounter after grade four are derivatives of familiar root words, and there are many root words that students typically need to acquire each year (research suggests between 600 and 1200) in order to adequately grow their vocabularies (Lehr et al. 2004).

The instructional solution is to teach students how roots combine with prefixes and suffixes, and provide some limited direct instruction in a few common root words, while emphasizing incidental instruction as described by Graves:

> If certain roots come up repeatedly in the material students are reading – as might be the case in a science class – then teaching these roots is likely to be worthwhile. Also, if older students want to learn non-English roots as part of their 'personal approach to building vocabulary' ... they should certainly be encouraged to do so (p. 111).

If teachers are going to provide direct instruction in some roots, it has been suggested to introduce Greek roots before Latin roots because their meaning is more obvious, and it is easier to see how they combine with other word parts (Edwards et al., 2004). Figure H is a list of common roots for teachers to use as a starting point.

Figure H

Common Greek Roots

Root	Meaning	Example
aero	air	aerodynamic
anthropo	human being	anthropology
astro	star	astrology
auto	self	autobiography
biblio	book	bibliography
bio	life	biology
chron	time	chronology
crat	rule	autocrat
dem	people	democracy
geo	earth	geology
graph	write, record	photograph

homo	similar	homogeneous
hydro	water, liquid	hydrodynamic
macro	large	macroeconomics
meter	measure	thermometer
micro	small	microscope
pathos	feelings of pity or sorrow	sympathy
phone	sound	telephone
photo	light	photosynthesis
psych	mind	psychology
scope	instrument for observing	telescope
tele	distance	telegram
theo	god	theocracy
therm	heat	thermometer
zoo	animal	zoology

Common Latin Roots

Root	Meaning	Example
amicus	friend	amicable
aqua	water	aquatic
aud	hear	audible
bat	to beat	combat
cred	believe	credible
dic/dict	say	diction
fend	to ward off	defend
fid	trust, have faith	fidelity

flect	bend	reflect
form	shape	formation
grad	step	gradual
grat	pleasing	gratify
jud/jur/jus	law	judiciary, jury, justice
lumen	light	luminous
mis/mit	send	transmission, transmit
mort	to die	mortal
ped	foot	pedestrian
pel, puls	push, drive	propel, pulse
plac	make calm	placid
port	carry	portable
rupt	break	rupture
scrib/script	write	inscription
spect	look, see, observe	inspect
spire	breathe	perspire
struct	build, form	construct
tract	pull, drag	tractor
vert, verse	turn	convert, reverse
vid/vis	see	video, visual

Step 4 Summary

An important component of good vocabulary instruction is directly teaching two strategies for inferring the meaning of unfamiliar words: how to use the context, and how to use knowledge of word parts. While the context does not always provide clues to meaning, there are times when the surrounding words and sentences do offer contextual clues in the form of definition, description, synonym, comparison, contrast, or example. For word analysis, there are three types of word parts that can be taught: prefixes, roots, and suffixes. It is particularly helpful to teach students the most common prefixes and how roots form the base for derivative words.

NOTES:

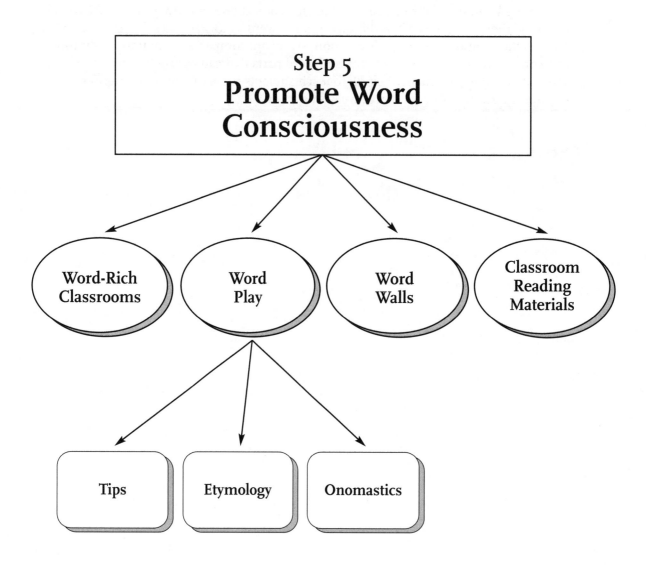

Step 5: Promote Word Consciousness

Developing word consciousness means helping students become interested in words on both a cognitive and an emotional level (Anderson & Nagy, 1992). Word conscious teachers share their enjoyment of learning new words and believe that students can learn how to enjoy the study of words. A word conscious classroom is full of unusual, interesting new words. Word consciousness also includes playing with words to make jokes, puns, word riddles, and tongue twisters (Lehr et al., 2004). Graves (2006) describes word consciousness as having an interest in learning and using new words, and becoming more skillful and precise in word usage. He points out that promoting word consciousness is an essential way to motivate some students to read and build their vocabularies.

Creating a Word-Rich Classroom

Beck, McKeown and Kucan (2002, 2004) suggest that a key ingredient to successful vocabulary instruction is a teacher who is an active, enthusiastic vocabulary learner:

> The teacher should be a partner in word awareness and discovering new words and new uses for words. The teacher can tempt students with words by giving them a new word to find out about or dropping clues to a word's meaning in creative ways.... Frequent impromptu attention to vocabulary can help instill in students a feeling of the power of words and the value of knowing words (p. 26).

They call this "enriching the verbal environment." This includes creating classroom conversations where words are valued as interesting and important, and classrooms that are "rife with words." They offer these suggestions for promoting word consciousness:

- Instruct students to keep a record of words they have learned, perhaps in the form of a personal word journal, or on a classroom bulletin board.

- Encourage students to make connections with new words outside the classroom. Challenge students to find words outside of class in books, newspapers, or on radio and television. When students find a word and share how the word was used, record it on a large chart in the classroom. For older students, finding words outside of class can be required or for extra credit.

- Use mature language and sophisticated words when talking to students and replace simple terms with more precise ones. Teachers should not avoid using difficult words because they think students might not understand. In this way, teachers become models for how unique words can be used.

- Ask students to identify or create a situation that can be described by a new vocabulary word. This can be done individually or in small cooperative groups.

- Create a suggestion box for students to place possible words for expanding the classroom word pool.

- Share with students your favorite words, how you recently learned a new word, or how you had a misunderstanding about a new word.

- Use current events as a source for interesting words.

- Provide resources in the classroom for learning about new words, including a user-friendly dictionary and thesaurus.

- Find opportunities to make connections between words that share the same roots, prefixes, or suffixes, and generate a word family derived from a new word.

Word Play

Blachowicz and Fisher (2004) note that research supports using word play in the classroom. Word play is motivating for word learning, causes students to reflect on words and be active learners, and is critical to the development of word awareness. Graves (2006) describes word play in this way:

> Words and phrases can simultaneously feel good on the tongue, sound good to the ear, and incite a riot of laughter in the belly. Verbal phenomena such as homophones and homographs; idioms, clichés, and puns; and onomastics (the story of names) offer myriad opportunities for investigating language (p. 123).

The term logology is used to refer to all forms of word and language play with the English language (Johnson et al., 2004).

Tips for Word Play

There are numerous books available at the library or in bookstores that can be used for word play in the classroom. Another resource for word play material is the internet. Websites abound with free games, lesson plans, and classroom activities. Here are a few suggestions:

- 50 Coolest Online Tools for Word Nerds: http://www.onlineuniversities.com/blog/2010/05/50-coolest-online-tools-for-word-nerds/
- A Word A Day: http://www.wordsmith.org/
- My Vocabulary.com: http://www.myvocabulary.com/
- Wordle: http://www.wordle.net/

The following search terms can also be used to find word play material:
- Homophones (words that have the same sound but different spelling) and homographs (words that have the same spelling but different meanings)
- Pun (a play on words or on different senses of the same word. Also, the similar sense or sound of different words)
- Word jokes and riddles
- Word category games (e.g., *Scattergories, Outburst*)
- Word picture games (e.g., *Pictionary*)
- Acting out word games (e.g., *Charades*)
- Synonym games (e.g., *Password*)

- Word learning games (e.g., *Scrabble*, *Boggle*)
- Word manipulations such as anagrams and palindromes
- Word expressions such as idioms, proverbs, and slang

Etymology

Etymology is the origin and historic development of a word. Discovering the earliest known use of a word, its changes in form and meaning, and its transmission from one language to another can be fascinating. There is a free online etymology dictionary available at *www.etymonline.com*.

Onomastics

Onomastics is the study of the origin and form of names. Johnson et al. (2004) have written a full book chapter about the different types of word play associated with names. They recommend the following books devoted to wordplay: *Names and Games* by R. Eckler (1986); *What's in a Name?* by P. Dickson (1996); and *The Dictionary of Word Play* by D. Morice (2001).

Word Walls

A word wall is an area on a blackboard, bulletin board, or wall space that is devoted to visually displaying words. While word walls are often used to support phonics concepts and spelling, they are also an excellent way to promote word consciousness in the classroom and develop vocabulary knowledge. The key to getting the most out of word walls is to use them often and update them frequently.

Content words to be taught in depth are excellent candidates for a word wall. Because these words are on display, teachers are more likely to refer to them often and they will be better remembered by students.

There are a number of games and activities that can be used with word walls. Here are some recommended resources for ideas for planning word wall lessons:

- Education World - Word Wall Resource Page: http://www.education-world.com/a_lesson/lesson/lesson328b.shtml

- Teachnet.com - Interactive Word Wall: http://www.teachnet.com/lesson/langarts/wordwall062599.html

- Florida Department of Education and Just Read, Florida - Word Wall Reading Strategy of the Month: http://forpd.ucf.edu/strategies/stratwordwalls.html

Classroom Reading Materials

In Chapter 2, it was noted that wide reading is a primary way for students to acquire new vocabulary. The amount students read is strongly related to their vocabulary knowledge. Nagy et al. (1987) estimate that from 25 to 50 percent of annual vocabulary growth can be attributed to incidental learning from context while reading. A word conscious classroom should have a wide variety of books and other material available about many different topics. This reading material will be the source for encountering new words.

Free Rice

One final suggestion to help students become more word conscious is to direct them to visit the website Free Rice (www.freerice.com). This website lets visitors build vocabulary through word quizzes and pledges to donate rice to the U.N. World Food Programme for each correct definition. The site provides a word with four possible definitions, and the words get more difficult as the game goes on. The website was created by an American computer programmer, John Breen. The rice is paid for by the advertisers whose names appear at the bottom of the webpage.

Activity: Practice Planning

Directions: Work with a partner to complete the following steps.

Step 1: Describe any school-wide activities that are being used to promote word consciousness.

_____

_____

_____

Step 2: Describe any classroom activities that you use to promote word consciousness.

_____

_____

_____

Step 3: Create two activities for promoting word consciousness that you can try with your students.

1. _____

_____

_____

2. _____

_____

_____

Step 5 Summary

If students believe that learning new vocabulary is tedious, difficult, and boring, they will be much less likely to see the value of learning new words. It is essential for teachers to provide a word-rich classroom and make students aware that discovering new words can be fun. Word play, word walls, and a classroom with a wide variety of reading materials are some of the ways to promote word consciousness.

NOTES:

Reproducible Templates

The Key Vocabulary Routine

1. Preview for difficult vocabulary
   - Identify problematic words, phrases, figurative language
   - Generate a previewing list
   - Provide background knowledge about the words to aid in comprehension while reading

2. Use activities that connect vocabulary to background knowledge and related words
   - Categorizing
   - Semantic Mapping
   - Semantic Feature Analysis
   - Scaling

3. Select specific words to teach in-depth
   - Identify a small set of key content words
   - Teach all aspects of the words
   - Develop user-friendly definitions

4. Identify opportunities to teach word learning strategies
   - Use of context to determine word meaning
   - Use of word parts to determine word meaning

5. Promote word consciousness

Word Knowledge Checklist

Word	Know it well, can explain it, and use it	Know something about it, can relate it to a situation	Have seen or heard the word	Do not know the word

Adapted from: Beck, I.L., McKeown, M.G., & Kucan, L. (2002). *Bringing words to life: Robust vocabulary instruction.* New York: The Guilford Press.

Semantic Mapping

Adapted from: Heimlich, J.E., & Pittelman, S.D. (1986). *Semantic mapping: Classroom applications*. Newark, DE: International Reading Association.

Categorizing

Words

_____   _____   _____

_____   _____   _____

_____   _____   _____

_____   _____   _____

_____   _____   _____

_____   _____   _____

_____   _____   _____

_____   _____   _____

Options for Categories

1. _____

2. _____

3. _____

4. _____

Semantic Feature Analysis

Words	Features					

Adapted from: Baldwin, R.S., Ford, J.C. & Readance,J.E. (1981). Teaching word connotations: An alternative strategy. *Reading World,* 21, 103-108.

Johnson, D.D., & Pearson, P.D. (1984). *Teaching reading vocabulary.* (2nd ed.). New York: Holt, Rinehart, and Winston.

Scaling

Adapted from: Moats, L.C. (2005) *LETRS: Module 4 the mighty word: building vocabulary and oral language.* Longmont, CO: Sopris West

Frayer Method

Concept Word: _____

Define the word, include picture if possible	List key characteristics and attributes
Example	**Non-example**

Adapted from: Frayer, D.A., Frederick, W.D., & Klausmeier, H.J. (1969). *A schema for testing the level of concept mastery* (Technical Report No. 16). Madison: University of Wisconsin, Wisconsin Center for Education Research.

Concept Definition Map

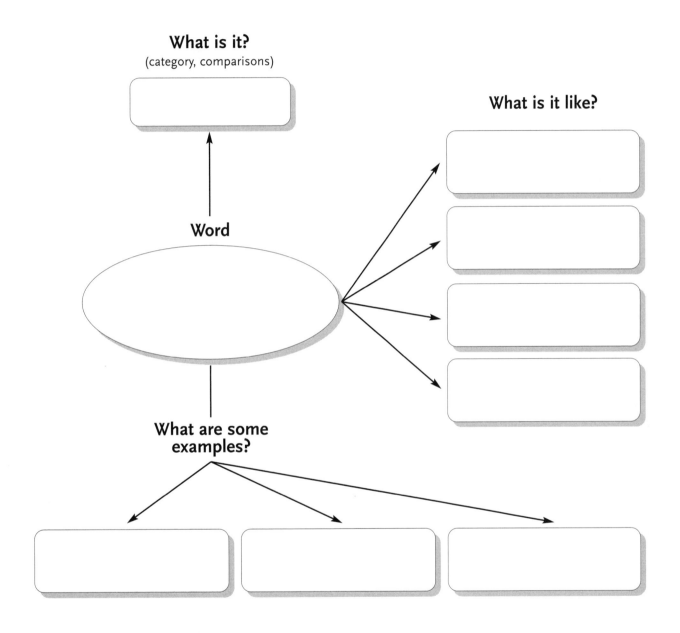

What is it?
(category, comparisons)

What is it like?

Word

What are some examples?

Adapted from: Schwartz, R.M. (1988). Learning to learn vocabulary in content area textbooks. *Journal of Reading, 32,* 108-118.

Two-Column Notes Template

_____	Definition:
	Part of speech:
	Synonym:
	Antonym:
	Category/related words:
	Example:
	Non-example:
	Multiple meanings:
	Sentence:
	Illustration:
_____	Definition:
	Part of speech:
	Synonym:
	Antonym:
	Category/related words:
	Example:
	Non-example:
	Multiple meanings:
	Sentence:
	Illustration:

Question Words

adapt	describe	infer	relate
agree	design	integrate	repeat
analyze	develop	invent	rephrase
apply	differentiate	interpret	represent
appraise	disagree	judge	rewrite
arrange	discriminate	label	select
assess	discuss	list	show
associate	dispute	match	simplify
calculate	dissect	measure	solve
categorize	distinguish	model	substitute
choose	divide	modify	summarize
clarify	elaborate	name	support
classify	estimate	omit	tabulate
compare	evaluate	order	tell
complete	examine	organize	test
compile	explain	outline	theorize
compose	experiment	paraphrase	use
conclude	extend	plan	utilize
connect	find	predict	what
contrast	formulate	prepare	what if
construct	generalize	produce	when
convince	generate	propose	where
create	give examples	quote	which
criticize	identify	rank	who
decide	illustrate	rearrange	why
defend	imagine	recall	
define	implement	recognize	
demonstrate	improve	recommend	

Transition Words and Phrases

To indicate a time relationship	after, afterward, after that, at first, at this time, before, beginning with, beyond, during, earlier, ending with, eventually, finally, following, from then on, in the meantime, last, later, meanwhile, next, now, since, soon, then, until, while
To indicate spatial placement	below, beside, between, beyond, farther on, here, next to, parallel with
To list or present a series of ideas	after, after that, finally, first, lastly, next, second, third
To add information or continue a line of thought	also, another, besides, further, furthermore, in addition, likewise, moreover, similarly
To summarize or show conclusion	accordingly, finally, in conclusion, in other words, in short, to conclude, to sum up, to summarize
To show comparison	by comparison, compared to, in like manner, likewise, similarly
To show contrast	although, but, however, in contrast, nevertheless, on the contrary, on the other hand, unlike
To repeat information or stress a point	above all, in fact, in other words, most important, once again, to repeat
To provide an example or illustrate a point	for example, for instance, such as, to illustrate, that is
To show cause and effect	as a result, because, because of, caused by, consequently, for that reason, that is why, therefore, thus
To state the obvious	certainly, granted that, in fact, most certainly, naturally, obviously, of course, surely, undoubtedly, without a doubt

Common Prefixes

prefix	common meaning	examples
un-	1. not 2. opposite of, contrary to	1. unhappy 2. unrest
re-	1. again, anew 2. backwards, back	1. rebuild 2. react
in-, im-, ir-, il-	1. not	1. inactive, immobile, irrational, illegal
dis-	1. not 2. opposite of 3. remove	1. dissimilar 2. disfavor 3. discolor
en-, em-	1. put or go into or onto 2. to cause to be	1. encage, embed 2. endear, emblaze
non-	1. not	1. nonhuman
in-, im-	1. into, inside, within	1. inbound, immerge
over-	1. above, too much	1. overuse
mis-	1. bad, wrong 2. failure, lack	1. misconduct 2. misfire
sub-	1. below, under 2. secondary 3. less than complete	1. subsoil 2. subplot 3. subhuman
pre-	1. before, in front of	1. prehistoric
inter-	1. between, among	1. international
fore-	1. before, in front of	1. forerunner
de-	1. make opposite of 2. remove 3. reduce	1. decriminalize 2. dethrone 3. declass
trans-	1. across, beyond 2. change 3. through	1. transatlantic 2. transcribe 3. transfer
super-	1. above, over 2. superior 3. excessive	1. superimpose 2. superfine 3. supercharge
semi-	1. half 2. partial 3. happening two times during	1. semicircle 2. semiconscious 3. semimonthly
anti-	1. opposite, counteracting	1. antigravity, antibody
mid-	1. middle	1. midstream
under-	1. beneath, below, less in degree	1. underage

THIS PAGE MAY BE REPRODUCED

Numerical Prefixes

Meaning	Greek	Latin	Examples
one	mono	uni	monotone, unicorn
two	di	bi, du, duo	dioxide, binoculars, duet
three	tri	tri	triangle, triplicate
four	tetra	quad (quart)	tetrahedron, quadruplets, quarter
five	penta	quint	pentagon, quintet
six	hexa	sext	hexagon, sextuplets
eight	octo	octo	octopus, octagon
ten	deca	deci	decathlon, decimal
hundred		cent	century
thousand	kilo	mille	kilometer, millenium
part, half	hemi	semi	hemisphere, semicolon
many	poly	multi	polygon, multifaceted

Adapted from: Ebbers, S. (2006). *Linking the language.* Self-published

Common Suffixes

Suffix	Meaning	Example
-able/-ible	capable of	believable, collectible
-al/-ial	pertaining to	personal
-ance	state or condition	performance
-ant	one who (occupation), a condition	consultant, compliant
-arium	a place for	aquarium
-ate	quality of, to act upon	literate, calculate
-cian	one who	musician
-ee/-eer	one who	employee, volunteer
-ent	causing an action, one who	absorbent, student
-er/-or	one who, that which	pitcher, inspector, clipper
-ful	full of	joyful
-ic	relating to or marked by	academic
-ion/-tion/-sion	a thing, noun; condition of	companion, intuition, passion, invasion, promotion
-ish	pertaining to, being	brownish
-ism	belief system, doctrine, practice	communism
-ist	believer in a system, doctrine	anarchist
-ity	state, quality of	abnormality
-ive/-tive/-ative	performing or tending toward a specific action	demonstrative
-ize	to cause to be or make	dramatize
-less	without	childless
-logy/-ology	study of	biology
-ly	resembling, having the quality of	happily
-ment	result of an action or process	excitement
-ness	quality or state of	softness
-ous, -ious, -cious	full of, having	joyous, curious, delicious

Common Greek Roots

Root	Meaning	Example
aero	air	aerodynamic
anthropo	human being	anthropology
astro	star	astrology
auto	self	autobiography
biblio	book	bibliography
bio	life	biology
chron	time	chronology
crat	rule	autocrat
dem	people	democracy
geo	earth	geology
graph	write, record	photograph
homo	similar	homogeneous
hydro	water, liquid	hydrodynamic
macro	large	macroeconomics
meter	measure	thermometer
micro	small	microscope
pathos	feelings of pity or sorrow	sympathy
phone	sound	telephone
photo	light	photosynthesis
psych	mind	psychology
scope	instrument for observing	telescope
tele	distance	telegram
theo	god	theocracy
therm	heat	thermometer
zoo	animal	zoology

Common Latin Roots

Root	Meaning	Example
amicus	friend	amicable
aqua	water	aquatic
aud	hear	audible
bat	to beat	combat
cred	believe	credible
dic/dict	say	diction
fend	to ward off	defend
fid	trust, have faith	fidelity
flect	bend	reflect
form	shape	formation
grad	step	gradual
grat	pleasing	gratify
jud/jur/jus	law	judiciary, jury, justice
lumen	light	luminous
mis/mit	send	transmission, transmit
mort	to die	mortal
ped	foot	pedestrian
pel, puls	push, drive	propel, pulse
plac	make calm	placid
port	carry	portable
rupt	break	rupture
scrib/script	write	inscription
spect	look, see, observe	inspect
spire	breathe	perspire
struct	build, form	construct
tract	pull, drag	tractor
vert, verse	turn	convert, reverse
vid/vis	see	video, visual

Key Vocabulary Activities Reflection Template

Name: _____

Date of lesson: _____

Description of class/students:

1. Which activity from *The Key Vocabulary Routine* did you try?

2. Describe the lesson that incorporated the activity.

3. How did the students respond?

4. Will you try this lesson again?

5. How might you improve the lesson/activity?

Bring a copy of the lesson/activity and student work samples to the meeting.

References

References

Allen, J. (1999). *Words, words, words: Teaching vocabulary in grades 4-12*. York, ME: Stenhouse.

Anderson, R. C. (1977). The notion of schemata and the educational enterprise: General discussion of the conference. In R.C.Anderson, R. J. Spiro, and W. E. Montague (Eds.). 1984. *Schooling and the acquisition of knowledge*. Hillsdale, NJ: Lawrence Erlbaum.

Anderson, R.C., & Nagy, W.E. (1992). The vocabulary conundrum. *American Educator, 16* (4), 14-18, 44-47.

Anderson, R.C. & Pearson, P.D. (1984). A schema-theoretic view of basic processes in reading. In P.D. Pearson, R. Barr, M. L. Kamil, & P. Mosenthal (Eds.), *Handbook of reading research*. New York: Longman.

Armbruster, B.B., & Nagy, W.E. (1992). Vocabulary in content area lessons. *The Reading Teacher, 45* (7), 550-551.

Baldwin, R.S., Ford, J.C. & Readance, J.E. (1981). Teaching word connotations: An alternative strategy. *Reading World, 21*, 103-108.

Baumann, J.F., Edwards, E.C., Boland, E.M., Olejnik, S., & Kame'enui, E.J. (2003). Vocabulary tricks: Effects of instruction in morphology and context in fifth-grade students' ability to derive and infer word meanings. *American Educational Research Journal, 40* (2), 447-94.

Baumann, J.F., Kame'enui, E.J., & Ash, G. (2003). Research on vocabulary instruction: Voltaire redux. In J. Fllod, D. Lapp, J.R. Squire, & J. Jenson (Eds.), *Handbook of research on teaching the English Language Arts* (2nd ed.). Mahwah, NJ: Lawrence Erlbaum.

Beaumann, J.R., Edwards, C., Boland, E.M., Olejnik, S., & Kame'enui, E.J. (2003). Vocabulary tricks: Effects of instruction in morphology and context on fifth-grade students' ability to derive and infer word meanings. American Educational Research Journal 40 (2), 447-494.

Beaumann, J.F., Font, G., Edwards, E.C., & Boland, E. (2005). Strategies for teaching middle-grade students to use word-part and context clues. In E.H. Hiebert and M.L. Kamil (eds.). Teaching and learning vocabulary: Bringing research to practice. MahwaH, NJ: Erlbaum.

Beck, I.L., & McKeown, M.G. (1985). Teaching vocabulary: Making the instruction fit the goal. *Educational Perspectives, 23*(1), 11-15.

Beck, I.L., & McKeown, M.G. (1991). Conditions of vocabulary acquisition. In R. Barr, M. Kamil, P. Mosenthal, & P.D. Pearson (Eds.), *Handbook of reading research, 2*, 789-814. New York: Longman.

Beck, I.L., & McKeown, M.G. (2007). Different ways for different goals, but keep your eye on the higher verbal goals. In R.K. Wagner, A.E. Muse, & K. R. Tannenbaum (Eds.). Vocabulary acquisition: *Implications for reading comprehension*. New York: The Guilford Press.

Beck, I.L., McKeown, M.G., & Kucan, L. (2002). *Bringing words to life: Robust vocabulary instruction*. New York: The Guilford Press.

Beck, I.L., McKeown, M.G., & Omanson, R.C. (1987). The effects and uses of diverse vocabulary instructional techniques. In M.G. McKeown & M.E. Curtis (Eds.). *The nature of vocabulary acquisition*, 147-163. Englewood Cliffs, NJ: Lawrence Erlbaum.

Beck, I.L., Perfetti, C.A., & McKeown, M.G. (1982). The effects of long-term vocabulary instruction on lexical access and reading comprehension. *Journal of Educational Psychology*, 74, 506-521.

Biemiller, A. (2004). Teaching vocabulary in the primary grades. In James F. Baumann & Edward J. Kame'enui (Eds.). *Vocabulary instruction: Research to practice*. New York: The Guilford Press.

Billmeyer, R., & Barton, M.L. (1998). *Teaching reading in the content areas: If not me then who?* Aurora, CO: Mid-continent Regional Educational Laboratory.

Blachowicz, C.L.Z. & Fisher, P. (2004) *Building vocabulary in remedial settings: Focus on word relatedness*. Perspectives, 30, 1. The International Dyslexia Association.

Blachowicz, C.L.Z., & Fisher, P. (2004b) Keep the 'fun' in fundamental. In James F. Baumann & Edward J. Kame'enui (Eds.). *Vocabulary instruction: Research to practice*. New York: The Guilford Press.

Bos, C.S., & Anders, P.L. (1990). Effects of interactive vocabulary instruction on the vocabulary learning and reading comprehension of junior-high learning disabled students. *Learning Disability Quarterly*, 13(1), 31-42.

Bromley, K. (2002). *Stretching students' vocabulary*. New York: Scholastic.

Bromley, K. (2007). Nine things every teacher should know about words and vocabulary instruction. *Journal of Adolescent & Adult Literacy*, 50 (7), 528-537.

Carlisle, J. F., & Katz, L.A. (2005). Word learning and vocabulary instruction. In J. R. Birsh (Ed.). *Multisensory teaching of basic language skills*. Baltimore, MD: Paul H. Brookes Publishing Co.

Carlisle, J.F. (2007). Fostering morphological processing, vocabulary development, and reading comprehension. In R.K. Wagner, A.E. Muse, & K.R. Tannenbaum (Eds.). Vocabulary acquisition: *Implications for reading comprehension*. New York: The Guilford Press.

Carlisle, J.F. (2010). Effects of instruction in morphological awareness on literacy achievement: An integrative review. Reading Research Quarterly 45 (4) 464-487.

Chall, J.S. & Jacobs, V. A. (2003). *Poor children's fourth-grade slump*. American Educator, Spring, 2003. American Federation of Teachers.

Common Core State Standards, Appendix A (2010). National Governors Association and the Council of Chief State School Officers. Retrieved July 17, 2011 from http://www.corestandards.org/

Cunningham, A.E., & Stanovich, K. E. (1998). What reading does for the mind. *American Educator*, 22, 8-15.

Dale, E. (1965). Vocabulary measurement: Techniques and major findings. *Elementary English*, 42, 82-88.

Diamond, L. & Gutlohn, L. (2006). Vocabulary handbook. Baltimore, MD: Paul H. Brookes.

Dickson, P. (1997). *What's in a name? Reflections of an irrepressible name collector.* Springfield, MA: Merriam-Webster.

Dickson, S.V., Simmons, D.C., & Kame'enui, E.J. (1995). *Text organization: Curricular and instructional implications for diverse learners.* Eugene, OR: National Center to Improve the Tools of Educators.

Ebbers, S. (2006). *Linking for language.* Self-published.

Edwards, C.E., Font, G., Baumann, J.F., & Boland, E. (2004). Unlocking word meanings: Strategies and guidelines for teaching morphemic and contextual analysis. In James F. Baumann & Edward J. Kame'enui (Eds.). *Vocabulary instruction: Research to practice.* New York: The Guilford Press.

Forbes, E. (1960). *Johnny Tremain.* Boston: Houghton Mifflin.

Frayer, D.A., Frederick, W.D., & Klausmeier, H.J. (1969). *A schema for testing the level of concept mastery* (Technical Report No. 16). Madison: University of Wisconsin, Wisconsin Center for Education Research.

Frey, N. & Fisher, D. (2011). Modeling word solving. Vocabulogic blog post, May 1, 2011. Retrieved from http://vocablog-plc.blogspot.com/2011/05/modeling-word-solving-frey-fisher.html

Fukkink, R.G., & de Glopper, K. (1998). Effects of instruction on deriving word meaning from context: A meta-analysis. *Review of Educational Research, 68* (4), 450-468.

Gaskins, I.W. (1998). There's more to teaching at-risk and delayed readers than good reading instruction. *The Reading Teacher, 51* (7), 534-547.

Graves, M F. (2000). A vocabulary program to complement and bolster a middle-grade comprehension program. In B. Taylor, M. Graves, & P. van den Broek (Eds.), *Reading for meaning: Fostering comprehension in the middle grades.* Newark, DE: International Reading Association.

Graves, M.F. (2004). Teaching prefixes: As good as it gets? In James F. Baumann & Edward J. Kame'enui (Eds.). *Vocabulary instruction: Research to practice.* New York: The Guilford Press.

Graves, M.F. (2006). *The vocabulary book.* New York: Teachers College Press.

Graves, M.F., Juel, C., & Graves, B.B. (2004). *Teaching reading in the 21st century* (3rd ed.). Boston: Allyn & Bacon.

Haggard, M.R. (1982). The vocabulary self-collection strategy: An active approach to word learning. *Journal Reading, 26* (3), 203-207.

Hart, B. & Risley, T.R. (1995). *Meaningful differences.* Baltimore, MD: Paul H. Brookes Publishing Co.

Hayes, D.P., & Ahrens, M. (1988). Vocabulary simplification for children: A special case of "Motherese". *Journal of child language, 15,* 401.

Heimlich, J.E., & Pittelman, S.D. (1986). *Semantic mapping: Classroom applications.* Newark, DE: International Reading Association.

Hirsch, E.D. (2003). *Reading comprehension requires knowledge – of words and the world: Scientific insights into the fourth-grade slump and the nation's stagnant comprehension scores.* American Educator, Spring, 2003. American Federation of Teachers.

Hirsch, E.D. (2006). Building knowledge: The case for bringing content into the language arts block and for a knowledge-rich curriculum core for all children. *American Educator 30* (1). American Federation of Teachers.

Jensen, E. (2005). *Teaching with the brain in mind.* Alexandria, VA: Association for Supervision and Curriculum Development.

Johnson, D.D., Johnson, B.V.H., & Schlichting, K. (2004). Logology: Word and language play. In James F. Baumann & Edward J. Kame'enui (Eds.). *Vocabulary instruction: Research to practice.* New York: The Guilford Press.

Johnson, D.D., & Pearson, P.D. (1984). *Teaching reading vocabulary,* (2nd ed.). New York: Holt, Rinehart, and Winston.

Juel, C. & Deffes, R. (2004). *Making words stick: What research says about reading, 61, 6.* Alexandria, VA: Association for Supervision and Curriculum Development.

Kamil, M.L., Borman, G.D., Dole, J., Kral, C.C., Salinger, T., & Torgesen, J. (2008). *Improving adolescent literacy: Effective classroom and intervention practices: A Practice Guide* (NCEE #2008-4027). Washington, DC: National Center for Education Evaluation and Regional Assistance, Institute of Education Sciences, U.S. Department of Education. Retrieved from http://ies.ed.gov/ncee/wwc.

Kuhn, M.R., & Stahl, S. A. (1998). Teaching children to learn word meanings from context: A synthesis and some questions. *Journal of Literacy Research, 30,* 119-138.

Laflame, J.G. (1997). The effect of the multiple exposure vocabulary method and the target reading/writing strategy on test scores. *Journal of Adolescent and Adult Literacy, 40* (5), 372-381.

Landauer, T.K., & Dumais, S.T. (1997). A solution to Plato's problem: The latent semantic analysis theory of acquisition, induction, and representation of knowledge. *Psychological Review,* 104 (2), 211-240.

Lehr, F., Osborn, J., & Hiebert, E.H. (2004). *A focus on vocabulary.* Honolulu, HI: Pacific Resources for Education and Learning.

Marzano, R. J. (2004). The developing vision of vocabulary instruction. In James F. Baumann & Edward J. Kame'enui (Eds.). *Vocabulary instruction: Research to practice.* New York: The Guilford Press.

McKeown, M.G., & Beck, I.L. (1988). Learning vocabulary: Different ways for different goals. *Remedial and Special Education, 9,* 42-45.

McKeown, M.G., & Beck. I.L. (2004). Direct and rich vocabulary instruction. In James F. Baumann & Edward J. Kame'enui (Eds.). *Vocabulary instruction: Research to practice.* New York: The Guilford Press.

Miller, G., & Gildea, P. (1987). "How children learn words." *Scientific American,* 257 (3), 94-99.

Moats, L.C., (2005). LETRS: *Module 4 The mighty word: Building vocabulary and oral language.* Longmont, CO: Sopris West.

Morice, D. (2001). *The dictionary of word play.* New York: Teachers and Writers Collaborative.

Nagy, W.E. (1988). *Teaching vocabulary to improve reading comprehension.* Newark, DE: International Reading Association.

Nagy, W.E., & Anderson, R.C. (1984). How many words are there in printed school English? *Reading Research Quarterly,* 19, 304-330.

Nagy, W.E., Anderson, R.C., & Herman, R. (1987). Learning word meanings from context during normal reading. *American Educational Research Journal,* 24, 237-270.

Nagy, W.E., & Herman, P.A. (1987). Breadth and depth of vocabulary knowledge: Implications for acquisition and instruction. In M.G. McKeown & M.E. Curtis (Eds.), *The nature of vocabulary acquisition,* 19-35. Hillsdale, NJ: Lawrence Erlbaum.

Nagy, W.E., & Scott, J.A. (2000). Vocabulary processes. In M.L. Kamil, P. Mosenthal, P.D. Pearson, & R. Barr (Eds.), *Handbook of reading research,* (3), 269-284. Mahwah, NH: Lawrence Erlbaum.

National Institute for Literacy (2001). Put reading first: The research building blocks for teaching children to read. Jessup, MD: National Institute for Literacy.

National Reading Panel (2000). *Teaching children to read: An evidence-based assessment of scientific research literature on reading and its implications for reading instruction.* Bethesda, MD: National Institutes of Health.

Pearson, P.E., & Gallagher, M.C. (1983). The instruction of reading comprehension. *Contemporary Educational Psychology,* 8, 317-344.

Peterson, C.L., Caverly, D.C., Nicholson, S.A., O'Neill, S., & Cusenbarry, S. (2000). *Building reading proficiency at the secondary level.* Austin, TX: Southwest Educational Development Laboratory.

Pressley, M., Disney, L., & Anderson, K. (2007). Landmark vocabulary instructional research and the vocabulary instructional research that makes sense now. In Richard K.

Rosenshine, B., & Stevens, R. (1984). Classroom instruction in reading. In P.D. Pearson, R. Barr, M.L. Kamil, and P.B. Mosenthal (Eds.), *Handbook of reading research,* 745-799. New York: Longman.

Ryder, R.J. & Graves, M. F. (1994). Vocabulary instruction presented prior to reading in two basal readers. *The Elementary School Journal,* 95 (2), 139-53.

Samuels, S.J. (2002). Reading fluency: Its development and assessment. In Pacific Resources for Education and Learning (Ed.), *Readings on fluency for "A focus on fluency forum."* Honolulu, HI: PREL.

Schwartz, R.M. (1988). Learning to learn vocabulary in content area textbooks. *Journal of Reading,* 32, 108-118.

Scott, J.A., & Nagy, W.E. (1997). Understanding the definitions of unfamiliar verbs. *Reading Research Quarterly, 32.*

Scott, J.A., & Nagy, W.E. (2004). Developing word consciousness. In James F. Baumann & Edward J. Kame'enui (Eds.). *Vocabulary instruction: Research to practice.* New York: The Guilford Press.

Sedita, J. (1989). *The Landmark study skills guide.* Prides Crossing, MA: Landmark School.

Sedita, J. (2003, 2008). *The Key Three Routine: Comprehension Strategy Instruction.* Danvers, MA: Keys to Literacy.

Snow, C. (2002). (Chair). *RAND reading study group: Reading for understanding: Toward an R&D program in reading comprehension.* Santa Monica, CA: RAND.

Snow, C.E., & Kim, Y. (2007). *Large problem spaces: The challenge of vocabulary for English language learners.* In R.K. Wagner, A.E. Muse, & K.R. Tannenbaum (Eds.).Vocabulary acquisition: Implications for reading comprehension. New York: The Guilford Press.

Stahl, S. A. (1986). Three principles of effective vocabulary instruction. Journal of Reading, 29, 662-668.

Stahl, S.A. (1999). *Vocabulary development.* Cambridge, MA: Brookline Books.

Stahl, S.A. (2004). *Vocabulary learning and the child with learning disabilities.* Perspectives, 30, 1. The International Dyslexia Association.

Stahl, S.A., Richek, M.A., & Vandevier, R.J. (1991). Learning meaning vocabulary through listening: A sixth grade replication. In J. Zutell & S. McCormick (Eds.) *Learner factors/teacher factors: Issues in literacy research instruction,* 185-192. The Fortieth Yearbook of the National Reading Conference, Chicago, IL.

Stanovich, K. E. (2000). *Progress in understanding reading: Scientific foundations and new frontiers.* New York: The Guilford Press.

Texas Reading Initiative (2000). *Comprehension instruction.* Austin, TX: Texas Education Agency.

Tomlinson, C. A. (2003). Differentiating instruction for academic diversity. In J. M. Cooper (Ed.), *Classroom teaching skills,* 7th ed, 149-180. Boston: Houghton Mifflin.

Wagner, R.K., Muse, A.E., and Tannenbaum, K.R. (Eds.). *Vocabulary acquisition: Implications for reading comprehension.* New York: The Guilford Press.

White, T.G., Sowell, J., & Yanagihara, A. (1989). Teaching elementary students to use word-part clues. *The Reading Teacher,* 42,

Classroom Examples

Semantic Mapping Examples

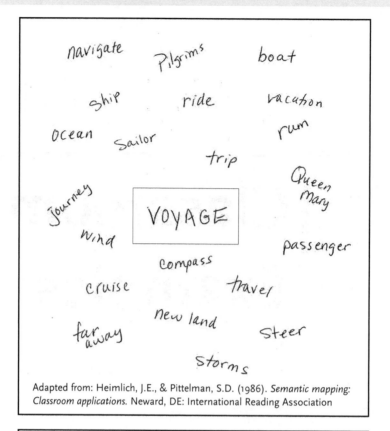

navigate   Pilgrims   boat

ship   ride   vacation

Ocean   Sailor   rum

trip

Journey   Queen Mary

VOYAGE

Wind   passenger

compass

cruise   travel

far away   new land   Steer

Storms

Adapted from: Heimlich, J.E., & Pittelman, S.D. (1986). *Semantic mapping: Classroom applications.* Neward, DE: International Reading Association

Slow

Slimy   rough

Small   hard

gross   Slithery   Soft

Shell   Camouflage

Smooth   fresh water   food

climate

tentacle   Snails   hibernate

mollusk   radula

gastropod   herbivore

dull

marshes   larvas   molusk

Outgrow   eye Stalk   bright

Adapted from: Heimlich, J.E., & Pittelman, S.D. (1986). *Semantic mapping: Classroom applications.* Neward, DE: International Reading Association

magma

igneous

weathering

metamorphic

erosion

pressure

$\left(ROCKS \right)$

lava

melting

sand

cooling

pebbles

clay

pressure

Semantic Feature Analysis Examples

Religions / Features	Major Leader	One God	Book of Laws/ Rules to Follow	Reincarnation	Promise of happiness/peace after death
Buddhism					
Christianity					
Hinduism					
Islam					
Judaism					

American Revolution

		pro-British	Anti-British	peaceful	violent	cause of revolution	effect of revolution	
loyalist		+	−	±	±	−	+	
patriot		−	+	±	±	±	+	
minutemen		−	+	−	+	−	+	
colonists		−	+	±	±	+	−	
protest		−	+	±	±	+	+	
tea party		−	+	+	−	+	+	
massacre		±	±	−	+	+	−	
revolution		−	+	±	+	±		
representative		−	+	+	−	±	+	

Geographic Features

	Contains water	has vegetation	has animal life	above sea level	above equator	surrounded by water	locally found	
valley								
plateau								
river								
tributary								
delta								
sea								
mountain								
hill								
lake								
volcano								
desert								
tundra								
mesa								
island								
penninsula								

	Can u see it?	Can u touch it?	Can it go in a glass?	Is it Liquid?	does it change the environment	does it change it's state of matter?
precipitation						
erosion						
evaporation						
condensation						
surface water						
ground water						
run - off						

	moving	still	fresh	salt	narrow	wide	shallow	deep
bog								
swamp								
sea								
lake								
ocean								
bayou								
levee								
delta								
river								
stream								
brook								
pond								

	benefits one	benefits more than one	harms one	harms more than one	depends on another
COMPETITION					
PREDATION					
SYMBIOSIS					
MUTUALISM					
COMMENSALISM					
PARASITISM					
PARASITE					
HOST					
PREDATOR					
PREY					

Poppy by Avi

Personality Traits	Characters					
	Poppy	Mr. Ocax	Ragweed	Lungwort	Cicely	Ereth
Courageous						
rebellious						
Sensitive						
ornery						
curious						
selfish						
controlling						

	Gaunt	Boisterous	Reproachful	Integrity	Intrepid	Intelligent	Good	Evil	Powerful	Trustworthy	Admirable	Loyal	Proud	Humble
Dorothy														
Scarecrow														
Tin Man														
Lion														
Wicked Witch														
Oz														
Glinda														

	fiction	non-fiction	public	private	paper	electronic	chronological
MEMOIR							
JOURNAL							
NOTE							
BLACKBERRY							
DIARY							
BLOG							

	equal sides	equal angles	parallel lines	perpendicular lines	acute angles	obtuse angles
POLYGON						
REGULAR POLYGON						
QUADRILATERAL						
ISOSCELES TRIANGLE						
EQUILATERAL TRIANGLE						
SCALENE TRIANGLE						

	Full length	Short	Casual	Dress up	Heavy material	Light material
Pants						
Slacks						
Trousers						
Capri						
Shorts						
Jeans						
Jams						
Sweats						
Wind pants						
Khaki						
Gouchos						

Kinds of Pants (Lesson for ELL Students)

	made of leather	has metal in it	used with stagecoach	used to ride a horse	used to direct horse
HARNESS					
HALTER					
TETHER					
RIBBONS					
BRIDLE					
REINS					
SADDLE					
BLINDERS					
BIT					
WHIP					

Name: _____

Date: _____

Planets of our Solar System

Features							
	Inner planet (1-4)	Outer planet (5-9)	Moons (0-2)	Moons (3-more)	Diameter Smaller than 13,000km	Diameter Bigger than 13,000km	Hot Cold
Planets							
Mercury							
Venus							
Earth							
Mars							
Jupiter							
Saturn							
Uranus							
Neptune							
Pluto							

Think about what you know about the planets in our solar system.

Write a plus (+) if a planet has the feature.
Write a minus (-) if the planet does not have the feature.

GEOGRAPHY OF VENEZUELA

	physical	cultural	economic	historical
PLANTATION				
OIL				
MESTIZOS				
ANDES				
CAUDILLO				
ANGOL FALLS				
ALTITUDE				
SIMON BOLIVAR				
SPANISH EXPLORERS				
ROMAN CATHOLIC				
GNP				
FOREIGN DEBT				
PETS				

	transparent	translucent	opaque
book			
wax paper			
folder			
dryer sheet			
window			
sheet protector			
instruction paper			
plastic ruler			
paint			
desk			

Scaling Examples

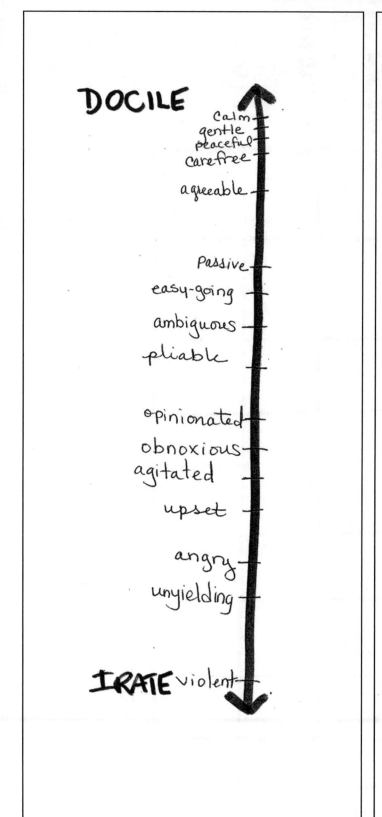

DOCILE

- Calm
- gentle
- peaceful
- carefree

- agreeable

- Passive
- easy-going
- ambiguous
- pliable

- opinionated
- obnoxious
- agitated

- upset

- angry
- unyielding

IRATE violent

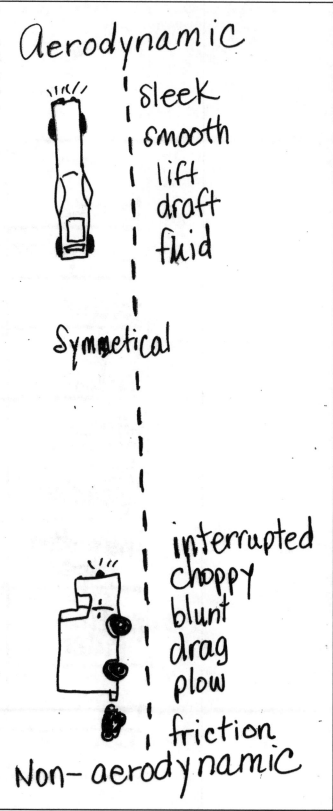

aerodynamic

- sleek
- smooth
- lift
- draft
- fluid

Symmetical

- interrupted
- choppy
- blunt
- drag
- plow

- friction

Non-aerodynamic

| introvert |

withdrawn
alone
timid
shy
dependent

social
well adjusted
well rounded
mature
evolved
independent
secure
confident
self assured

| extrovert |

intrepid invincible heroic conqueror

<u>courageous</u> - brave

    leader - general - soldier - decorated
      determined
        stoic
          strong

comfortable
at ease
relaxed

uncommitted

shy
timid
nervous
anxious
stressed
teary

<u>fearful</u>

frozen paralyzed scared agonizing terrified

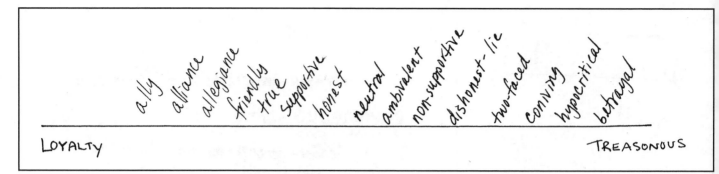

LOYALTY   TREASONOUS

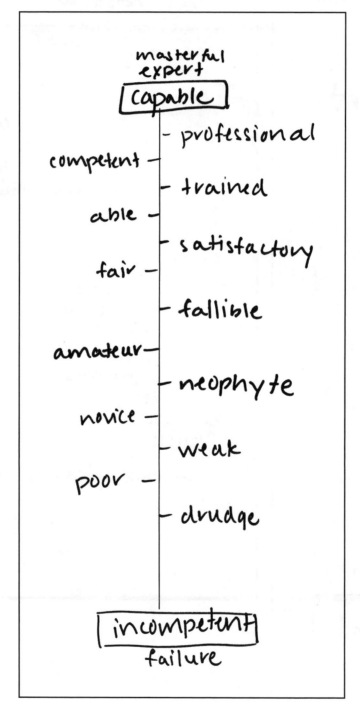

coarse

	rough
	prickly
	bumpy
	brittle
	husky
	uneven
	texture
	soft
	silky
	even
	pleasant
	slippery
	sleek
	glasslike
	flat

smooth

Because of Winn Dixie

suicidal
depressed
sorrowful
Melancholy ☹
numb
down trodden
sad / gloomy
unhappy
dissatisfied
negative
pessimistic
discontented
Calm 😐
content
even keeled
just right
satisfied
pleased
excited
optimistic
positive
happy 😊
bouyant
joyous
jubilant
ecstatic

transparent
clean
see through
light
bright
sheer
murky
cloudy

thin

translucent
stained glass
some light

paper
tinted

thick
dark
solid

opaque

The Giver

wayward
defiant
stubborn
rule breaker
rude
disrespectful
opinionated
fresh
disobedient
individualistic
indifferent

indulge
agreeable
placate
cater
rule follower
docile
obedient

Scaling

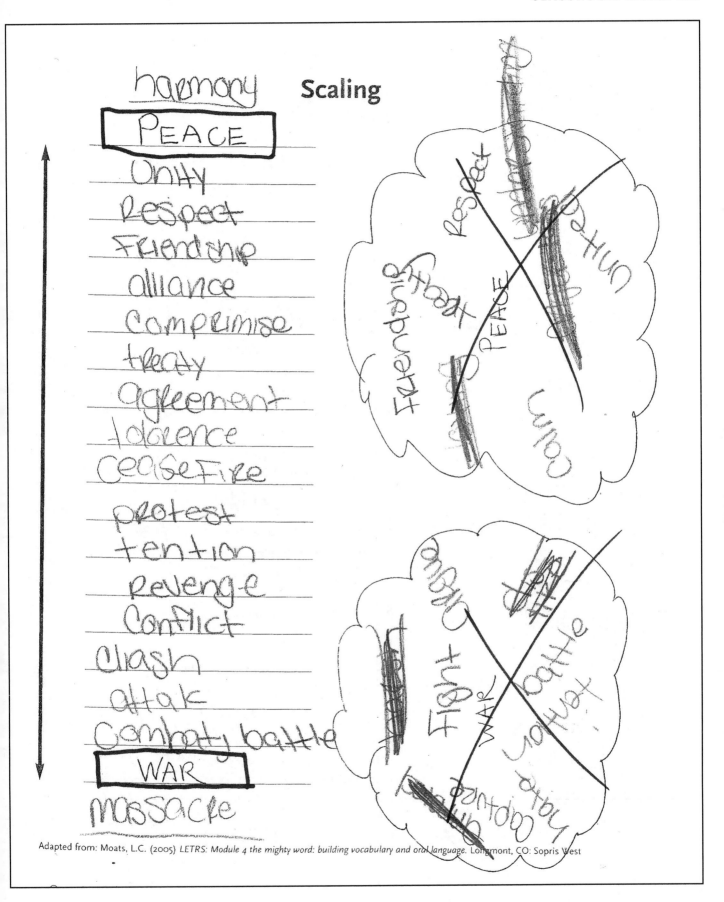

harmony

PEACE

unity

Respect

friendship

alliance

compromise

treaty

agreement

tolerence

ceasefire

protest

tention

revenge

conflict

clash

attak

combat/battle

WAR

massacre

Adapted from: Moats, L.C. (2005) *LETRS: Module 4 the mighty word: building vocabulary and oral language.* Longmont, CO: Sopris West

(delighted)
overjoyed
discouraged
downtrodden
saddened
elated
fornlorn
hopeful
frustrated
happy
anxious
ebullient
joyful
enthusiastic
jubilant
ecstatic
miserable
gloomy
deflated
dejected
Eeyore
sullen
(disappointed)

(passionate)
exuberant
tireless
driven
forceful
motivated
enthused
engaged
eager
exciteable
love
happy
neutral
flat
shy
dull
bored
stubborn
lifeless
noncommital
(passive)

Frayer and Four-Square Examples

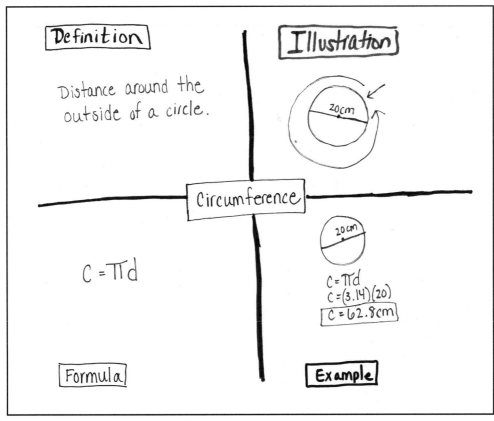

Definition

Distance around the outside of a circle.

Illustration

20cm

Circumference

Formula

$C = \pi d$

Example

20cm

$C = \pi d$
$C = (3.14)(20)$
$C = 62.8 cm$

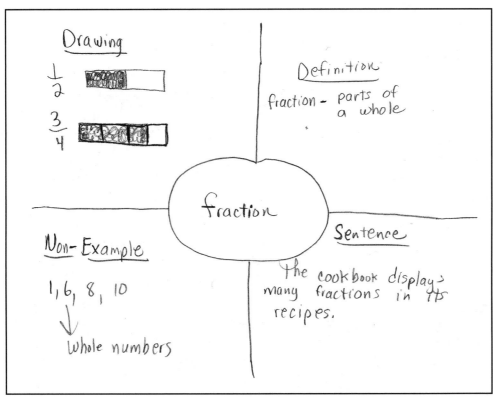

Drawing

$\frac{1}{2}$

$\frac{3}{4}$

Definition

fraction - parts of a whole

fraction

Non-Example

1, 6, 8, 10

↓

whole numbers

Sentence

The cookbook displays many fractions in its recipes.

Frayer Method

Concept Word: _alacrity_

Define the word, include picture if possible	List ~~key characteristics and attributes~~ Antonyms
liveliness briskness 	sluggish lethargic
~~Example~~ Synonyms	Non-example
eager spright excited	The student entered the room with alacrity because he was so happy for a short school day.

Adapted from: Frayer, D.A., Frederick, W.D., & Klausmeier, H.J. (1969). *A schema for testing the level of concept mastery* (Technical Report No. 16). Madison: University of Wisconsin, Wisconsin Center for Education Research.

The Frayer Model Map
On boisterous

DEFINITION:

noisy

loud

Stormy crazy

CHARACTERISTICS:

adjective

rough rowdy

screaming wild

boisterous

EXAMPLES:

Screaming kid
crying.
Dogs barcking
at a cat.
wild bear gowling
at a Dear.

**NON-
EXAMPLES:**

quiet

Laxing in a
quiet field
butterflys
flying.

Frayer Method

Concept Word: _____conundrum_____

Define the word, include picture if possible	List key characteristics and attributes
something that puzzles or causes confusion 2. [puzzle piece drawing] 2. 2. 2.	Confusion, mystery, puzzle, riddle, perplexes, anything that peeks curiosity
Example A math problem An anigma How to fix something	**Non-example** Exact answer Formula Knowing what you want to eat

Adapted from: Frayer, D.A., Frederick, W.D., & Klausmeier, H.J. (1969). *A schema for testing the level of concept mastery* (Technical Report No. 16). Madison: University of Wisconsin, Wisconsin Center for Education Research.

Word: Mass

Define the word, include picture if possible	List key characteristics and attributes
Mass describes the amount of matter in an object -Baseball -Mass 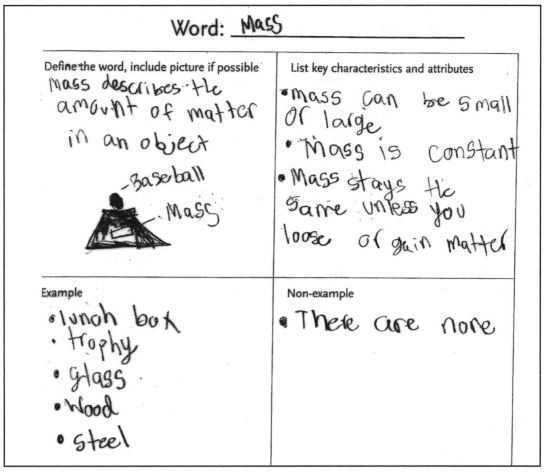	• mass can be small or large. • Mass is constant • Mass stays the same unless you loose or gain matter

Example	Non-example
• lunch box • trophy • glass • wood • steel	• There are none

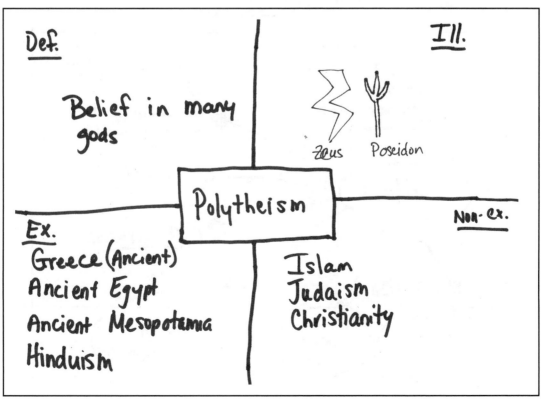

Def.   Ill.

Belief in many gods

Zeus   Poseidon

Polytheism

Ex.

Greece (Ancient)
Ancient Egypt
Ancient Mesopotamia
Hinduism

Non-ex.

Islam
Judaism
Christianity

Concept Definition Map Examples

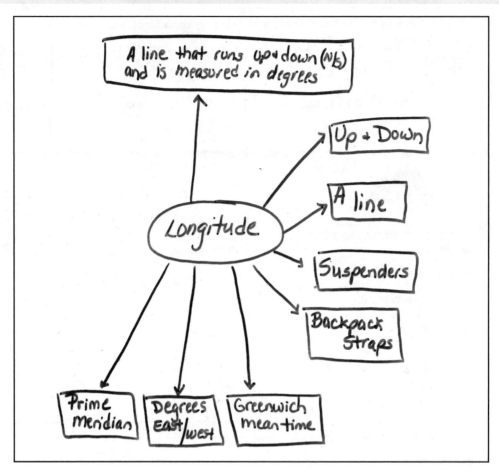

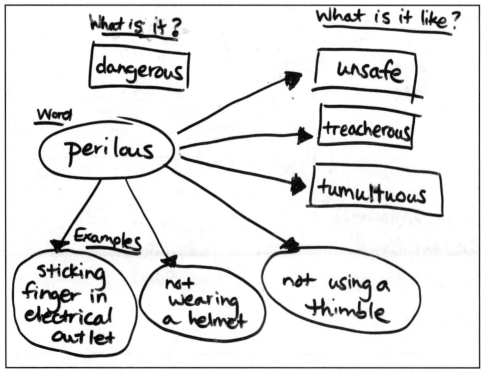

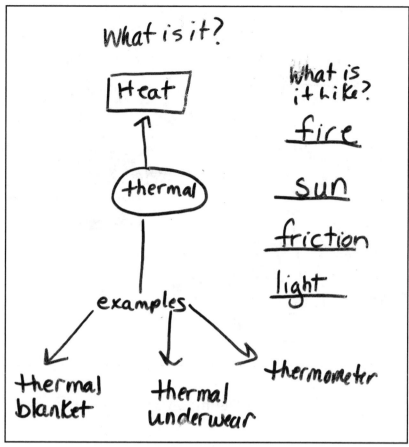

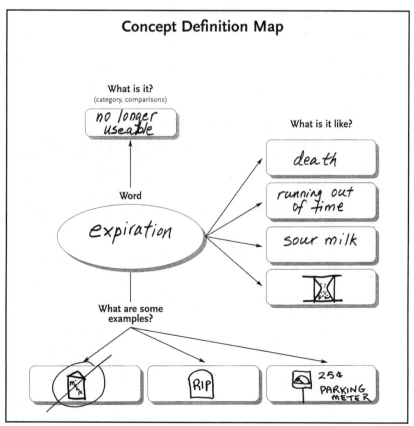

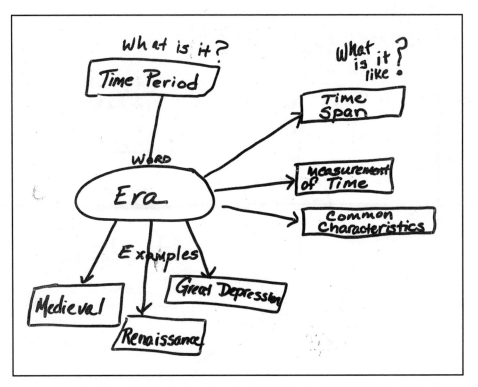

Concept Definition Map

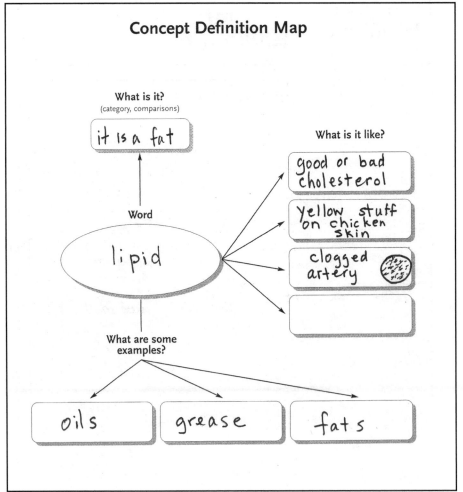

Two-Column Notes Examples

Melancholy	- a deep sadness
 	- synonyms: morose, depressed, in the dumps, downtrodden
 	- antonyms: happy, joyful, amiable, jubilant, exuberant
 	- categories: emotion, feelings, mood
 	After the death of his dog the boy was melancholy.

congruent ≈	DEF. having the same measure
	POS adjective
	SYN. same, equal
	ANT. noncongruent, unequal
	CATEGORY angles, triangles, polygons
	EX. equilateral triangle
	NON-EX. scalene triangle
	In an equilateral triangle, all angles are congruent.

hemisphere

Definition:
A sphere divided into two halves

Part of Speech:
Noun

Synonym:
Half a globe

Category / Related Words:
world, continents, equator, prime meridian

Example:
Northern & Southern Hemisphere

Multiple Meanings:
Part of the brain
Cerebral hemisphere

Sentence: The U.S. is in the Northern Hemisphere.

picture:

Modest

Definition: having a humble opinion of oneself or one's accomplishments

Part of speech: adjective

synonym: shy

antonym: pompous, confident, showy

category: personality trait

examples: Wilbur (Charlotte's Web)

non-example: Templeton

multiple meaning: modest income

sentence: Wilbur was a modest pig.

Value

definition: number amount

examples: 60°

non examples: immeasurable calculation.

multiple meanings: belief, feeling of importance

part of speech: noun

related words: degrees, more than, less than, equal

Categorizing Examples

Directions: Review the below list of vocabulary words. Create at least two categories that may be used to group some of the vocabulary words. Write the category and the words that support that category in space provided.

Vocabulary Words:

Absolute Value	Data	Difference	Title
Decimal	Horizontal Axis	Line Plot	Sum
Equation	Fraction	Probability	Product
Frequency Table	Simplify	Vertical Aix	Integers
Percentage	Tally Marks	Stem-and-leaf plot	

Vocabulary Words

1. abolitionists-people who were against slavery and worked to end it
2. burlap-a heavy, woven material that feels rough
3. conductor-a guide; someone who helped escaped slaves get to the North
4. customs-things that are past down from generation to generation
5. instincts-natural feelings about something
6. master-owner of the plantation;boss of the slaves
7. mistress-usually the plantation owner's wife
8. muskrat-a water rodent that has glossy brown fur and webbed feet
9. overseer-someone who worked on a plantation:to control the slaves
10. passionate-feeling something very strongly
11. plantation-a large farm in the South that produced crops for money
12. seceded-pulled out or withdrew from something;states that left the Union
13. survive-to stay alive
14. territory-an area of land outside a country's borders
15. Underground Railroad-the secret system for slaves to escape the North

Suggestions for Categories

People
Feelings
Words of the South
Misc.

Capítulo 6

Los Verbos	Los Colores (colores)	Como te Queda?	Los Precios (precios)	La Topa	Las Tiendas (tiendas)	Cuando?	La Cultura	
							Semejanzas	Diferencias
Buscar	Rojo	Median	Uno	Vestido	descuentos	hace	Centro	Caro
Comprar	Anaranjado		dos	Sudadera	ropa	dias	Commercial	Sastres
llevar	Rosado	Gerande	tres	sueter	zapateria	semanas	Marcas	
Pagar	Verde	Pequeno	cuatro	tenis	almacen	ano		
	Azu		Cinco	zapatos	Centro	mes		
	Marron		seis	pantalone	commertil	Ayer		
	Morado		Siete	cortos	supermercado	pasade		
	blanco		Ocho	falda		Manana		
	Negro		Nueve	blusa				
	amarillo		Diez	camisa				
	gris		Pagaste	camiseta				
			pague	pantalone				
			Compre	jean				
			Compuste	pantimedias				
			Caro	calcetines				
			Barato	vaqueros deportes				

SIGNAL WORDS FOR MATH OPERATIONS.

Directions: Cut and paste the signal word under the appropriate operation.

INCREASE	DISCOUNT	COMBINE	OF
TIMES	DIFFERENCE	PRODUCT	SPLIT
PLUS	PERCENT	SUM	HALF
DECREASE	SHARE	DIMISHED	MINUS
QUOTIENT	PER	EACH	MORE THAN
FEWER	ADDED	HOW MUCH LESS	DOUBLED
ALL TOGETHER	TAKEN AWAY	OUT OF	TAX
ADDED TO	TRIPLED	TOTAL	EACH
GAVE	INCREASED BY A FACTOR OF	HOW MUCH MORE	

ADDITION

MULTIPLICATION

Weather Words

Clouds	Temperature Scales	Precipitation Types	Storms
Cumulus nimbus stratus cirrus	Farenheit Celsius Centigrade	rain snow fog virga hail sleet drizzle	blizzard showers heat wave

Categorize these solar system words.

Andromeda
big dipper
Cassiopeia
day
Earth
Gemini
Jupiter
little dipper

Mars
Mercury
Neptune
Orion's Belt
Pleiades
Polaris
revolve
rotate

Saturn
Sirius
Sun
Uranus
Vega
Venus
Year

Constellations	Planets	Related to time	Stars
big dipper	Earth	day	Andromeda
Cassiopeia	Jupiter	revolve	Polaris
Gemini	Mars	rotate	Sirius
little dipper	Mercury	year	Sun
Orion's Belt	Neptune		Vega
Pleiades	Saturn		
	Uranus		
	Venus		

Primary Grades Examples

Crops

def: plants grown for food
part speech: noun
syn: season's growth
related words: produce, fruits, fields, farming
example: wheat, corn, soybeans
mult. mean: to cut short
Sentence: The farmer used his tractor in the field to grow his crops.
picture:

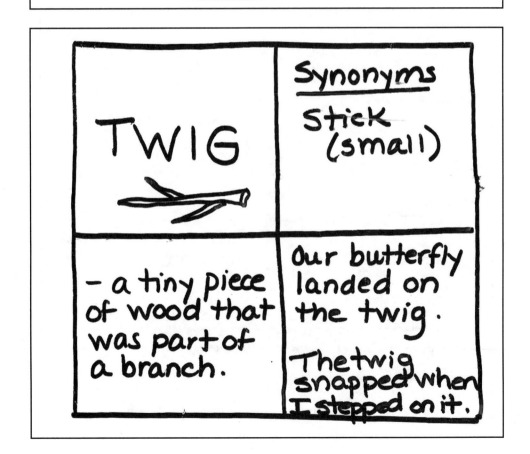

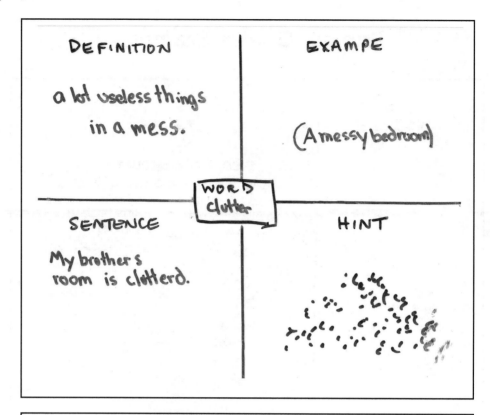

DEFINITION

a lot useless things
in a mess.

EXAMPE

(A messy bedroom)

WORD
clutter

SENTENCE

My brothers
room is cletterd.

HINT

Concept Word: is land

Define the word, include picture if possible

land surrounded by water
on all sides. p. 190

List key characteristics and attributes

1. ocean breeze
2. salty air
3. sandy beaches
4. bird habitat

Example

1. Martha' Vineyard
2. Nantucket
3. Block Island
4. Hawaii
5. Bahamas

Non-example

1. Cape Cod
2. Florida
3. X Island
4. harbor
5. Mountain
6. reservoir

Frayer Method

Concept Word: __residential__

Define the word, include picture if possible	List key characteristics and attributes
where people live 	• people's homes • sidewalks • lawns • playgrounds • neighborhood
Example • suburbs • apartment complex • gated community	**Non-example** • shopping malls • downtown • farm • beach • amusement park • busines buildings

Adapted from: Frayer, D.A., Frederick, W.D., & Klausmeier, H.J. (1969). *A schema for testing the level of concept mastery* (Technical Report No. 16). Madison: University of Wisconsin, Wisconsin Center for Education Research.

	herbivore	carnivore	fur	scales	feathers	mammal	amphibian	insects	water-dwelling	land-dwelling
RACCOON										
FOX										
FROG										
WHALE										
SEAGULL										
ANT										

	wide	narrow	flowing	distinct borders	salty	fresh	deep	shallow	tidal
STREAM									
BROOK									
CREEK									
POND									
LAKE									
RIVER									
OCEAN									

		wings	shell	6 legs	antennas	stinger
fly						
bee						
grasshopper						
mosquito						
cricket						
moth						
beetle						
ant						
spider						

Natural

Mountains
Rivers
Ocean
Lakes
Trees
Animals
Farm Products
Maple Syrup
Hiking Trails
State Parks
Tourist Attractions
Government
Cities/Towns

Man-made

Scaling

↑
standing still
crawl
trudged
creep
ambled
walk
speed walk
trotted
jog
run
sprinted
bolted
↓

Joshua   grade 2

Semantic Mapping

aliens   satellite

no gravty

                              galaxies

planets

Spaceship | Space |

                              moon

black

                stars

rover   astronaut

      earth

Adapted from: Heimlich, J.E., & Pittelman, S.D. (1986). *Semantic mapping: Classroom applications*. Newark, DE: International Reading Association.

Keys to Literacy®

About Keys to Literacy

Keys to Literacy is a professional development and consulting company specializing in comprehension and vocabulary instruction, content literacy instruction, adolescent literacy, and literacy planning.

What we do
We prepare schools and districts to improve student literacy and performance by training teachers on research-based literacy strategies to embed in their classroom instruction. Our instructional routines are based on the most current research and are recognized by teachers and administrators as fundamental, practical, concrete, useful, and effective.

Our professional development applies to all content areas and special education, and includes:

The Key Comprehension Routine   *The Key Vocabulary Routine*
ANSWER Key to Open Response   *Literacy Planning for Grades K-12*

Our Key Comprehension and Key Vocabulary training typically includes two initial days of teacher instruction by a Keys to Literacy trainer, or a hybrid combination of live and online training. These initial sessions are supplemented with a structured series of follow-up meetings, including small group coaching, guided practice, classroom modeling and observation. Schools are encouraged to choose building coaches who facilitate the implementation of the Key strategies and receive extra training to support their peer educators. We provide added support for these building coaches.

We also offer classroom materials to reinforce the strategies taught in *The Key Comprehension Routine* and *The Key Vocabulary Routine*. Implementation Portfolios are available for recording Key activities and to keep track of samples for future reference. Posters and laminated Student Guides give students easy to use tips to improve comprehension. In addition to our comprehension and vocabulary routines, we offer a one-day teacher workshop, *ANSWER Key to Open Response,* to help students perform better on standardized tests. Finally, we work with schools and districts to develop comprehensive literacy plans for grades K-12.

Who we are
Our staff of literacy experts has significant experience with K-12 literacy issues. We understand the reality of working in a school because we have been there as teachers and administrators. Our experience as educators has enabled us to develop instructional strategies that work because they are research-based, proven, practical, concrete, useful, and effective. We are dedicated educators who share a passion for improving student literacy skills by improving teacher strategies and instructional methods.

Contact Us
To learn more about Keys to Literacy, visit our website at www.keystoliteracy.com, call 978-948-8511, or email us at info@keystoliteracy.com.